A
BOOK
TEACHER
FOR EVERY
SCHOOL

A BOOK TEACHER FOR EVERY SCHOOL

Featuring Mount Kenya Academy

By Kemie Nix

Foreword by Ashley Bryan

Published by
Children's Literature for Children
2710 Woodland Brook Lane
Atlanta GA 30339
www.childrensliterature.org

in collaboration with

Peachtree Publishers
1700 Chattahoochee Avenue NW
Atlanta GA 30318-2112
www.peachtree-online.com

Design and composition by Melanie McMahon Ives

Printed in August 2016 by LCS Communications
10 9 8 7 6 5 4 3 2 1
First edition
ISBN 978-1-56145-990-2

Cataloging-in-Publication Data is available from the Library of Congress.

*To my students—all of you—from the Fulton County Juvenile
Detention Center, Atlanta Public Schools, The Westminster Schools,
Mount Kenya Academy, and Kenyan government schools—
including those of you who have lived with me:
Mary Evelyn, Johnny, Abi Joy, Steve, Krystle, Sophie, and Kate.*

*And to Barbara Harrison of the gentle greatness,
with deep gratitude for the sense of community and friendships
that she has fostered in the children's book world.*

Ashley Bryan (Photograph by Sarah Corson)

FOREWORD
By Ashley Bryan

Getting books to children changes lives. The books encourage reading and impart knowledge that allow the readers to better effect changes in the world. This will open to all the possibilities of becoming a contributing and creative force that will make a positive difference in their lives and ours—a glowing inspiration for all.

By going to Kenya and working with Mount Kenya Academy and government schools, Kemie Nix is a living example of what "Outreach" means. She is never held back by the magnitude of the challenges; she goes forward in working to get books into the hands of children, knowing that the best we have to offer is the best we can do.

Joining with Kemie in this project, by going to Kenya and working alongside her with the children, has given me a deeper insight into my work in retelling and illustrating the African folktales.

In thanks for the many gifts of these children, I have offered physical improvements to some of the poorest of the government schools to enhance their education. It gives meaning to our own lives when we reach out to help others.

When you also see the work that Charity Mwangi, the founder and director of Mount Kenya Academy, is doing to reach out to the schools that have so little, you are inspired by her brilliant leadership as an educator.

Every kind and thoughtful gesture has the potential to make the world a better place.

PROLOGUE
A Book Teacher
for Every School

When I began my work in the early sixties, I had the good fortune to be teaching at The Westminster Schools, where I had all the resources I needed plus a great deal of academic freedom. Westminster remains to this day an independent school in Atlanta serving students from grades pre-first (an academic kindergarten teaching beginning reading) through twelfth. During my time there, I would teach a grade level for a year or two and think, "Well, I've done that." Then I would switch to another grade level. After a decade, I had taught all of the elementary grades except second. Changing grade levels kept me engaged in the elementary curriculum and gave me insight into child development. I wondered what age would be my favorite, and it turned out that I enjoyed them all.

While teaching all of the subjects, reading was always my primary interest, and this sweeping approach to teaching gave me a practical overview of reading education for all grades. It was not inspiring: reading education during the 1960s had become reductionist. Children would read uninspiring stories in their basal textbooks specifically crafted for word count and vocabulary; these stories were accompanied by unimaginative questions to be answered orally in class and in writing on accompanying workbook pages. I noticed that few children, save the two or three dyed-in-the-wool bookworms in every class, were reading actual books.

About this time, verbal scores on the Scholastic Aptitude Tests for college entrance examinations fell one point at the national level. Our headmaster, Dr. William Pressly—an educator who could spot a trend before it had time to develop—began meeting with the faculties of our elementary, middle, and high schools to ensure that this ugly trend never darkened our doors.

I believed that there might be a connection between falling verbal scores and reading education at the elementary level. My experiences had shown me that the children were complying with the reading requirements of textbooks but appeared to have little interest in actual books. There was a wealth of excellent children's books in the elementary school library that seemed to be generally ignored. Over the years, I had pondered how to get children to read the outstanding literature available in schools and libraries. This seemed to be my window of opportunity. I went to Dr. Pressly with the idea of teaching children's literature to children by reading actual books instead of textbooks. My salary as a one-classroom teacher would have to go to the person replacing me in the classroom, and my new position would need to be funded as an additional teacher's salary. Dr. Pressly said, "I don't know if I have enough money, Kemie. Let me think about it." In a couple of days, he told me that I could try it for one year. I have never looked back.

The reading of books is the highest form of literacy. If a child can read books, all the lesser forms of literacy—reading articles, essays, and everything else—falls into place. If a child learns to love reading books, that child can be saved academically and frequently in other ways. (Even higher mathematical skills, which depend on a subtle understanding of prepositions, are fostered by excellent reading skills. That is why many young children who are good at computation but not at reading hit a wall at about fourth grade and usually cannot progress into higher mathematics.)

Once children have mastered decoding skills (skills that a child uses to make sense of printed words), the sooner they begin reading real books, the better. The Westminster Elementary School children's literature program began at the third grade level, when children had mastered these skills. It continued through sixth grade, the last grade in elementary school at that time.

I met with each class of approximately twenty-five students for an hour a week, spending about two-thirds of a class period on books, mythology, poetry, and projects, and one-third of the time in the library selecting and checking out books. I developed reading folders (paper folders containing dated diaries to record two weeks' worth of reading per page with a cumulative list of finished books at the front). Children were required to read forty-five minutes a night, five nights a week. If children missed a night for some reason or other, they were asked to check the "I did not read" box and write out the reason. They did not have to make up missed reading. "Watched television" or "Forgot" were not acceptable excuses. Later on, these reading records were easily transferred to computers by two friends who taught children's literature at the university level.

Over time, the children taught me that forty-five minutes was too long, so the time requirement was reduced to thirty minutes. (Nevertheless, this is valuable homework—unlike the usual and endless busy work.) It was a real uphill struggle to get everyone in third through sixth grade reading real books, but I persisted, telling the students that they could choose what books they wanted to read but they must read books. I introduced the students to as many fine books as possible through book talks, reading aloud, and encouraging the children themselves to share information about books. (Westminster students, however, were "Hurried Children" before this expression was coined. They were involved in so many after-school activities that one girl complained to me, "I can't read thirty minutes a night. I don't even have time to pet my dog!")

I discovered that there were two or three "resisters" in every class and two or three bookworms. In the beginning, the bookworms were not pleased to have to record their reading, but gradually they began to enjoy documenting their accomplishments and discussing good books with an adult who also appreciated their books. The program was most successful with the middle group of children, between the two extremes, who wanted to cooperate with their teachers and do their assignments. I expected continued struggle the second year of the program requiring the students to read real books, but to my great astonishment they had internalized the structure and requirements, and it was relatively easy to implement.

The children were asked specifically to read fiction for a number of reasons. Nothing develops long-range thinking skills like reading a work of fiction. Children must keep the characters, setting, and the plot in their memories over an extended period of time. (This helps to explain the great appeal of series books. The student has learned the personalities of the characters and can concentrate on the fun part—the plot. *Every* book a child reads is helpful. Reading speed will increase even if children read books in a series or books that are "too easy.")

While I greatly value nonfiction, especially biography and poetry, the author—the silent partner who teaches—is another crucial aspect of fiction. So many authors give children an empathetic understanding of themselves and others. When children recognize themselves through an emotional connection to a fictional character (human or otherwise), it can ease the loneliness and solitude that lie at the heart of every human. Most adults usually come to terms with being alone, but children experience it with intensity and they have little understanding that others might feel as they feel. When they grasp that someone else feels the same way, they respond by loving the book, perhaps without realizing that there is a real person behind the words.

Caring people can save children—but so can the authors of books if children find them somehow. Many successful adults who have come from harsh childhood backgrounds have given books the credit for saving them. Books have been the secret to their success. Some children blunder into books on their own, but with adult help, many more can be reached.

Recognizing that most troubled young people are poor readers, I tried to take as many good books as possible into Atlanta's Fulton County Juvenile Detention Center, and trusted the authors to reach hearts. For more than twenty-five years, Trudy Green, a fellow member of Central Presbyterian Church in Atlanta, and I volunteered there.

The first book that a child feels an emotional connection with and truly loves, I have dubbed the "Aha! book." I will never forget leaving a copy of Katherine Paterson's *The Great Gilly Hopkins* for an incarcerated girl. When I returned the following week, she shouted out, "I am Gilly!" That was her "Aha! book." Sometimes, the "Aha! book" is the very first book a child reads. Sometimes, it takes consistent help for a long time to find the right book for the right child, but it is a worthy goal.

Books of poems also have great "Aha!" power. Children love poetry. Poems have the ability to connect with a child's heart, partly because of their brevity. "Catching on" to the meaning of a poem delivers a small "Aha!" moment, as do the pleasures of rhythm and rhyme.

Consistently requiring that real books be read with assistance (and with support of individual book preferences) over a number of years almost always brings children to a love of books. This is why parents are so successful at fostering a love of books in their children (not to mention the kindness and attention involved). Inconsistency, however, is built into our present educational system, where children change teachers every year.

As for the wonderful book-loving teachers themselves, and most are, they are increasingly burdened and are grateful for all the help they can get. Most school media specialists do yeoman's duty, trying to help children consistently throughout their school careers, and they are responsible for many a book-loving adult as well. But books are only a part of their responsibilities, and a shrinking part at that. (Not all media specialists are good at their job, unfortunately. I have worked *with* fine media specialists whose students have received a double dose of enthusiasm for books; I have also worked *around* poor media specialists where at least one person was standing in the breach.) A classroom teacher or school media specialist *can* foster a love of books in a year. People *can* discover a love of books any time in their school careers—or lifetimes, for that matter—but that is leaving an important life skill to chance. The sooner people learn to love books, the better.

Once people learn to love these masterpieces of

information and understanding, it does not matter in what direction their individual tastes and needs take them. They now have the master key to the door of enhanced future lives.

After I had been working with the reading program for a few years at Westminster, I wondered if it would work at the other end of the economic spectrum. I couldn't solve the social problems of economically deprived children, but perhaps I could help to alleviate an educational problem.

During this time Mary Amos, another member of Central Presbyterian Church, was seeking volunteers to tutor one child weekly at Ed S. Cook Elementary School in the Capitol Homes housing project. With "illusions" of grandeur, I decided, "Shoot, I will tutor the whole school." Working with the principal Betty Strickland (who later became superintendent of the Atlanta Public Schools), I arranged to teach all of the classes from third through fifth grades on Mondays. This was a total of eight classes. I had been toughened by my years of volunteering with incarcerated young people, so I wasn't concerned about potential behavioral problems from a few of the economically deprived children.

Like Westminster students, most of the children at Cook Elementary School had also mastered the decoding skills by third grade. I began to teach the exact same curriculum at Cook that I was teaching at Westminster, and I largely succeeded. However, I discovered that I had no bookworms in any class, and a few more resisters per class. Once again, I found the program succeeding with the large middle group of cooperative students, and we began to develop some bookworms. (Two absolutely sterling teachers, Helen Wilson and Ethel Jennings, embraced the program and helped their students enormously in learning to love books.) The resisters read books too.

Media specialists and teachers wear different mantles. The former are in the business of offering books. But as a teacher I could say, "You *are* going to read books. It is your assignment." Considering all the vast technological advances eating up children's time, I believe that someone needs to speak for books consistently.

One problem at Cook, however, was the poor quality of the books available. I knew that the Westminster students had buckets of books, so I started a program asking children to give, not their old cast-off books, but two or three of their favorite books that they were willing to share. Thus, the Reader-to-Reader project was born. (It began expanding beyond the inner city almost immediately, and we have given well over two million books globally.) By this time, all of my friends and relatives were running from me because I always needed money. My Aunt Adah said that she wasn't giving me another dime until she could take it off her income tax. I applied for nonprofit 501(c)(3) status and the project officially became Children's Literature for Children, the redundant but descriptive title. I also became the children's book editor of the *Atlanta Journal-Constitution* and later, *Parents' Choice* magazine (the nation's oldest nonprofit reviewer of all children's media and toys), so I had many review copies to share.

I planned to wait until I had elementary school graduates before evaluating the program. But after a couple of years, the reading scores were improving at Cook, and Dr. Alonzo Crim, the superintendent of Atlanta Public Schools, took an interest in the program. (The most intimidating class that I ever taught happened one day when I was working in a fifth grade classroom. The door flew open, and Dr. Crim and his entourage came in, arranged themselves along the wall, and listened to the lesson in progress.) While I could not take credit for the improved reading scores, because many people were working very hard to help, I was a factor.

Dr. Crim, who was a fine educator and became a good friend, asked me to implement the program at Campbell Elementary School in an even more challenging housing project in Atlanta, Carver Homes. (Someone once asked me if I was afraid to work in Carver Homes, and I said, "No, because criminals don't get up at 7:30 in the morning.") Westminster gave me a sabbatical to work in these two urban schools, Cook and Campbell. With this additional school, I really wanted to get the statistics for my program, and I went to the research and evaluation department of Atlanta Public Schools asking them to evaluate the program. The head of the department liked the idea and assured me that they would evaluate it. I asked him to please pretest and then wait three years to posttest when most of the students had participated in the children's literature program for three years. He enthusiastically agreed, and I trusted him. I have mercifully forgotten his name.

I worked for three years, and in the spring of my third year at Campbell, I went back to the head to get my statistics. He told me that they had not pretested. In fact, they had done nothing whatsoever. I was crushed and cried all weekend. Then I pulled myself together and asked myself who was the top reading person in the country. I thought it was Dr. Jeanne Chall at Harvard University, so I called her. She agreed to see me, and I went to Boston and met with her. She liked the program and told me that I *was* getting results, but I just wasn't getting *at* the results, and she gave a number of suggestions. I followed up with some of the people she had suggested, but nothing seemed to pan out. (Dr. Chall liked the program so much that she became an Advisory Board member, and continued in that position for the rest of her life.)

Dr. Chall also asked me the essential question, "What is it that you really want?"

I answered, "A book teacher for every school."

One teacher who consistently requires and supervises the reading of books throughout the years of students' elementary school careers can have a long-term positive impact on literacy. That teacher, however, must genuinely love both children and their books because that love is contagious. (You can't catch the flu from someone who doesn't have the flu.) By this time, I knew that one person could affect the literacy of an entire school. It also seemed like common sense to me, but I had no statistics to back me up.

All of this essay implies linear progress of this program. In the interest of brevity (you may be thinking, "Too late"), I have left out all of the fits and starts and dead ends as the program developed. Also, no one can claim success for an educational program until the children have grown up and can report on it. Multitudes of my former students have participated in children's literature and become adults.

Ask my alumni.

I cannot leave out the invaluable help from volunteers, to whom I am eternally grateful. Inadequate but heartfelt thanks are due to *ALL*, but especially to the earliest volunteers: Caroline Lathan at Cook Elementary School; Dale Thompson, Susan Lipsitch, Jeanne Hicks, Beverly Hurt, Susan Kimmey, Comfort Owusu, and Gail Goodwin at Campbell. Before she moved away, Charlotte Kelley helped me enormously at a critical stage of development and gave me my motto: "Finish one thing before you start another." (Charlotte sits on my shoulder to this day repeating this mantra. Sometimes, it even works.) All these volunteers began coming on board as the inner-city work expanded. I know that a children's literature program can be implemented by one teacher, but the more people helping children read books, the better. Volunteers and the children themselves have been my very best teachers.

The help from these volunteers led to new support from the other side of the world when Charity Mwangi, the headmistress of Mount Kenya Academy in Nyeri, Kenya, was visiting The Westminster Schools. Dale Thompson, a parent at Westminster who innocently had said to me one day, "Kemie, let me know if I can help you," and promptly got drafted into working at Campbell, insisted that Charity visit our program at Campbell, which she did. She saw its value, and she invited me to implement it in Kenya. I immediately stopped trying to prove what I already knew and turned my attention to Africa.

Next, I applied for and received a grant with which I bought duplicate copies of many fine books, one for Mount Kenya Academy and one to give to another school.

When I was ready to distribute these duplicates elsewhere, I discovered that Kenyan children in most government schools had no books. Instead, they worked in pamphlets and had never even seen or held a book. I became determined to extend Reader-to-Reader to Africa. Any school can start a library if they have a bookshelf. Now everyone I knew or met was finagled into sending books to Africa. We began libraries at many government schools.

On one of my trips, I invited the author-illustrator Ashley Bryan to come along. We visited a number of schools where we had begun libraries, and Ashley adopted the poorest one in a remote arid area: Kiboya Primary School. First Ashley donated the money to buy water tanks to capture rainwater so the children would have clean water to drink. Next he funded the Ashley Bryan Library at Kiboya, thus inspiring the brick-and-mortar aspect of Children's Literature for Children. Through the generosity of many people, we have funded more than twenty-five water tanks for government schools, built over a dozen libraries, several classroom buildings, and some kitchens. We have also provided uniforms for the students of a few schools. (This is something that I particularly like doing, because it provides work for local women.)

Also, Judy Grimes, another dear friend, was working as a chaplain at a children's hospital in Atlanta. She and I talked of the importance of stories in helping to alleviate the stress of hospital settings and medical procedures for young patients. We set out to help mitigate this problem to some extent, and the Reader-to-Patient program was born. Many volunteers have worked in and helped establish this vital outreach program. Special thanks go to Susan Hawkins and Janet Peck who helped get it off the ground. It has now been implemented both in the United States and Kenya at hospitals serving children. Wanja Thairu directs Reader-to-Patient in Kenya.

Of course, there are worlds of children who listen to and love stories—humanity has a story-loving gene. Many simply don't have access to books. If books become available, however, the stimulation of imagination, the artistry of diverse artists, ideas, and adventures that they cannot have in their small bodies also become available.

Children's Literature for Children (CLC) now uses books as a gateway to help children in *any* way that we can.

Please visit our website at *www.childrensliterature.org*.

INTRODUCTION
Adventures in Kenya

In 1989, in addition to observing at Westminster, Charity Mwangi visited Children's Literature for Children at Campbell Elementary School in Carver Homes. In this one short visit, we could see that we were simpatico in our educational approaches and personalities. The next afternoon, Linda Grady, a pre-first teacher at Westminster and the first teacher to visit Mount Kenya Academy, gave a party for Charity and I attended. At this party, Charity invited me to bring my program to her school. I said that I would love to. I then went home in a high state of excitement to convey the news to my husband John. Wanting to study more about Africa, I perused my bookshelves and noticed for the first time how loaded my shelves were with books about Africa and African animals, not books about Europe or China, for example, just Africa. How curious.

I was invited to teach for a year. Although our children were grown, teaching for a year was too long to be away from home. Hashing out the dilemma with John, he suggested that

I go for one term, basically three months, and added, "If you like it, you can always go back."

Thus began twenty years of visiting Mount Kenya Academy for teaching stints lasting a few weeks to a few months. I had always stayed with the hospitable Charity and her husband Charles. To have me as a houseguest for long stretches of time required incredible kindness and patience, which they displayed in abundance. Betty, their daughter who was away at college in England, had a bedroom on the ground floor in which I lived.

Not knowing what books or resources I would find at Mount Kenya Academy, I had bought books and materials to take with me, planning to implement the program in the same manner I had used in the United States—requiring students to read books, helping them to find appealing books, and requiring them to record their reading. As a result of being a visiting teacher over the years, I was privy to an insider's view of the phenomenal growth of Mount Kenya Academy. Much as I loved and appreciated my years of teaching at Westminster, the twenty years at this strong and unique African institution (by Africans, for Africans) were the most rewarding of my professional life.

They were also great fun. I hope that the wonderful experiences I enjoyed are conveyed through the following collection of letters. In those pre-blogging days, I typically mailed my letters to John and he made copies and sent them out to an assortment of friends and relatives. Some letters were to my dear friend, the author Lloyd Alexander, who had saved them in his correspondence files. While I had not had the foresight to save copies of the letters myself, his files contained them all. I made copies of my own letters in January, 2010, while visiting Brigham Young University's official opening of "Lloyd's Box"—his office, which he gave to the university upon his death. They recreated it in a special seminar room in the large children's section of their main library. Brigham Young University also houses Lloyd's correspondence and memorabilia, thanks to the good offices (and friendships with Lloyd) of Jim Jacobs and Mike Tunnell, both children's literature professors at Brigham Young.

Because most of the letters have a salutation of "Dear Friends and Relatives" and usually end with "Love, Kemie," I'm going to dispense with those repetitions and just move from one date to the next like a diary. Any inaccuracies or offenses against anyone are purely my own foolishness, and I beg the forgiveness of the annoyed in advance. My great affection for my readers then and now is a given.

Establishing the very first library at Muruguru Primary School

CHAPTER ONE
1990

January 15, 1990

"Jambo!"

I'm sitting in the lobby of the New Stanley Hotel in Nairobi waiting for Charity Mwangi. I spoke with her on the phone yesterday, and she's picking me up at the hotel. It's 11:00 AM here and 3:00 AM EST. If you're interested in what time it is here, add eight hours to your time—remembering Kenya is ahead of the United States. Staying at the hotel for the first couple of nights is a good way to get over jet lag.

After lunch yesterday, I decided to venture out to see if I could learn my way around Nairobi. It was easy and reassuring to see a lot of police. Many con games were going on. I understand that you have to bargain in Kenya—which I don't enjoy. I know I've got to learn how, but it makes me uncomfortable. I always feel like the rich trying to rob the poor. There is also an element of respect involved—people don't seem to respect you if you pay too much money for something. (Happy, yes—respect, no.) But in a con game, nobody respects anybody—competitive from the get-go.

Americans are proud of their shoes—or, at least, I seem to be. The streets are lined with shoe shiners. When they called out "Madame, Madame," I ignored them. One young man hooked me with, "What kind of shoes are those? May I just look at them?" I adore my black Easy Spirit shoes (black leather sneakers)—and I let him see them. Another guy came out of the woodwork and started feeling my shoes. Due to my naiveté, I now had two strange men feeling my feet. They asked me how much they cost in U.S. dollars. I told them $70. Then we were all three appalled—them at the cost, me at my embarrassing acknowledgment to have paid that much. Before the afternoon was over, I could tell who the entrepreneurs were. They were the ones who begged to see my wonderful shoes. (I'm sure they were dazzled, but I was much too ashamed to ever again admit how much they cost.)

It was thrilling to see my first mosque. I heard a man calling from the prayer tower. I studied the courtyard and didn't see a single woman, so I just stood outside the gates and admired as much of the mosque as I could see and tried to decide if the man in the tower was a talented caller or had a loudspeaker...loudspeaker, I decided. The shoe shiners at the gates asked if I wanted to know what he was calling, and I said, "Yes."

They told me that he was calling, "You are welcome here, please come in." I thought he was probably saying, "Any foreign she-devil—especially one in trousers—who sets her foot in here will never be seen again."

Nairobi has the feel of a town. The poverty is an overwhelming first impression—but the second impression is of vitality and color.

January 15, 1990 (another letter)

While waiting for Charity, I keep watching the groups of khaki-covered tourists being shepherded around, and it makes me glad that I'm alone—relatively speaking. I was mighty glad to have the company of John Prichard and Rich Rodman, liaisons to the Presbyterian Church East Africa (PCEA) from the U.S. Presbyterian headquarters, while getting a taxi to the hotel at 1:30 AM. We landed at 11:00 PM, and it took us two and a half hours to get through the airport. I met John and Rich in the Amsterdam airport, where I was looking for two Presbyterian ministers, one older and one younger. I overlooked John because he was smoking like a chimney. I finally approached them. John was thin with gray hair. He had smoke wrinkles and smelled like tobacco. With all the smokers I have loved in my life, starting with my father, I like the smell of tobacco and was predisposed to like him. They were both very nice—John was a definite extrovert, and I admired his style while dealing with Kenyan customs' red tape. Rich was quieter and was doing what I was doing—observing.

While the first overwhelming impression to my eyes is poverty, I think that the eyes adjust rapidly. The streets looked normal to me this morning when I sallied forth. Yesterday, I sometimes noticed what seemed to me to be overall shabbiness. The air and sunshine are fabulous.

John and Rich just passed me on the street, John wearing a hot pink shirt. They were supposed to fly to Addis Ababa this morning at 8:30 AM. I didn't see them yesterday, so I wrote them a goodbye note and taped it to their door. As I was wandering down the street, I thought I heard someone call, "Kemie" (pronounced "Kamie"). Not knowing a soul in Nairobi, I dismissed the notion that someone was calling me—until I heard my name called a second time. They got bumped from their plane and will have to try again tomorrow. We went for tea, and Rich said that in the U.S. they would have been furious.

January 15, 1990 (10:00 PM)

Good grief, what a day! Someone dented Charity's car— so while her husband Charles and some government official that he had drafted went to the freight terminal to free the forty boxes of books and supplies I had brought, Charity and I, and another man who works at the school, drove around the industrial section looking for Economy Shoes. The culprit who bashed her car worked for that company. I saw a section of the city I never would have seen otherwise— shacks, goats, and poverty along the roadside, but also an enormous amount of work and building going on behind the "roadside strip." When we finally gave up and went back to

24

the freight terminal, these two highly competent men had been unable to get my boxes out of the customs warehouse. We had to spend the night in Nairobi, so Charles and Charity decided to spend the night at "The Club." I was so interested in everything I was seeing that I paid little attention to the plans. Charles drove off in the school truck with the two men, and Charity and I took the dented car.

It wasn't until I was *inside* the club that I realized it looked familiar. I am staying in my own suite of rooms at the Muthaiga Country Club—the club that Beryl Markham and Karen Blixen frequented—the club in the movie *Out of Africa*. Charity said that Africans have not been allowed to be members until recently.

We had a drink in the bar and ate in the dining room with pink tablecloths, flowers, candles, wine. It couldn't have been lovelier. When I was getting dressed for dinner, looking at my reflection in the mirror in the bedroom of my suite with two private bathrooms, I thought of all the romantic evenings that have begun and ended there.

Charles seems to know everyone in Kenya. He is a famous entrepreneur. As for me, I shouldn't be let out of the house. I promptly ate a salad, which I had been warned not to do, and I've already been bitten by a mosquito.

January 20, 1990

So much has happened that I don't know where to begin. I guess I'll start with Mount Kenya Academy. The classroom buildings are built of red bricks that are the size of concrete blocks in the United States but are much more attractive. The concrete floors are painted a red-brick color. It is sparse but open and airy with the windows open to the sunshine and breezes. There are green fields and flowers. The school goes from Standard One through Standard Eight (grades) with approximately twenty-five students in each class. The students are African and Indian—about evenly divided between boarding students and day students. They are very appealing and attractive running around in uniforms.

Charity took me into the office and introduced me to the staff. Miss Esther is Charity's secretary and, like most school secretaries, she reigns over the school. A cute little fat boy came into the office and listened intently to everything. Charity then took me around the school, pointing out all of the various features. The child followed us everywhere with seemingly no concern about his school schedule. After about an hour of looking at the school, I finally inquired, "Who is this cute little fat boy who keeps following us around?"

Charity said, "You didn't know that he is my nephew, Thomas?"

The other children have been eyeing me too, and a few brave ones have sidled up to me in the library where I am unpacking the boxes that it took Charles two days to spring from customs. I have been trying to process the books in order to start teaching classes next week.

I have had a couple of "woozy" spells while leaning over boxes, and when I have tried to sleep at night, I can hear my heart pounding in my ears. I puzzled over that until I realized that I am around seven thousand feet above sea level and not used to it. Everyone says I should be acclimated in about a week. Charles, who obviously doesn't suffer fools kindly, said to stop worrying (meaning, stop talking) about the altitude—so I did.

The weather is glorious—cool, crisp nights with sweaters and fires, and warm breezy days. Although we are right at the equator, we are so high that it is eternally springtime with a profusion of flowers everywhere. Both Charity and Suzanne Whitfield, a woman who grew up in Atlanta but moved with her husband to Kenya in the early seventies, have large country gardens with a welter of colors and flowers. I've seen beautiful gardens—but not like these.

Charles and Charity have three children. The two girls, Betty and Wandia, are in college in England, and their son, Tony, is in college in Pennsylvania. The Mwangis' house is large and sprawling. I am ensconced downstairs, and their bedroom is upstairs. When we came home from school yesterday, I actually heard African drumming off in the distance. It continued for a long time. Charity's home is a few miles from school over extremely bumpy roads. My overall impression of the school is that the children are disciplined and happy. They are hardworking too. Mount Kenya

Academy scored tenth in the nation academically last year, and seventh this year—which is phenomenal considering the school's small size.

Friday night, Charles, Charity, and I ate dinner with Suzanne and Randy Whitfield in their large, comfortable, English-style country home. The house is impressive with large rooms, parquet floors, many dogs, and a fire in the fireplace. Two couples in the Peace Corps elsewhere in Africa were there, so I found the conversation fascinating. Have you ever noticed that everyone's work consists chiefly of problems? It's just that some problems are interesting and some are boring. Peace Corps problems are not boring. Because Randy and Suzanne are from Atlanta and both attended Westminster, the conversation occasionally turned to "Do-you-knows?" Randy's mother, Shirley, was my Aunt Adah's great friend, so I had seen Randy a number of times over the years.

When I have been listening to conversations not in English, I have assumed that I was listening to Kiswahili. It turns out that I am listening chiefly to Kikuyu. I hear English expressions sprinkled in, however, such as "Okay."

Earlier today, we went gliding—or rather two of the school's best students went gliding. The top scorers on the Kenya Certificate of Primary Education tests, Joyce and Tabitha, were taken gliding as their reward. Before they went aloft, they looked a little dubious about their reward, but they were smiling after they landed. (Perhaps in relief.) There were too many people for me to go, but I am going back on a less busy day to go gliding. The countryside is so beautiful from the ground I can hardly stand it—let alone from the air.

Suzanne took us to a farm to see the warthogs. Apparently, one of her friends who owns a large farm found an injured warthog and nursed it back to health. The patient returned to the bush and told all of his friends and relatives about this "soft touch." A worker arrived with a large bucket of huge grains of corn. She called, "Piggy, Piggy." All of these wild warthogs appeared as if by magic out of the bushes and fields. The babies came too. Apparently, jealousy is not confined to humans. Across the yard, Mama Warthog was nuzzling one of the babies, and the little fella by me was watching this exchange of affection. He started whimpering, which increased in volume until Mama heard it and came over and nuzzled him too. I was startled when a huge, wild (but not very) boar complete with tusks trotted up, cocked his head, and examined me out of his beady eye.

January 21, 1990

My plan to stay off of caffeine was a farce. I am now gulping down innumerable cups of very strong tea daily. At school, they serve large (so large I can hardly lift them) kettles of strong, sweet, milky tea. The kitchen staff works so hard that I wouldn't dream of asking for special tea. When in Rome...

People who live in Nairobi and the Central Highlands of Kenya grow many types of food. The soil in many fields is rich, black volcanic soil. It is an agricultural society, and food seems to be plentiful—at least this year. There is also a bright red soil that I assume is clay. It reminds me of Georgia clay.

Charity and her husband Charles live in a spacious house. Like the Dutch, we take off our shoes upon entering the house. When I inquired about why we were doing it, it turns out to be for the same reason as the Dutch—to keep from tracking mud into the house during the rainy season. At school, I was interested to see the children's shoes all lined up at the front of the classrooms.

Charles's accent is a little hard for me to understand. It took us a couple of days to understand each other. He has a sly sense of humor, and he is never serious. After discovering that I have no knowledge of cows, he gave me a stick "for protection," and we went off to see his cows. I was afraid that I might meet a snorting bull. We walked up to a herd of gentle, benign-looking cows, and I said, "These are *Jerseys!*" He laughed and asked me how I knew. I told him that my daughter, Mary Evelyn, had lived on the Isle of Jersey where I had visited her, and Jerseys were probably the only cows on the planet that I could identify.

Fruits, especially bananas, are very plentiful, and there is even a finger-size sweet banana. At breakfast on Friday, I said, "I'll just have a little banana."

Charles said, "Since I am from a banana republic, I will eat a large banana." He also tickles me because he doesn't suffer in silence. We ate dinner at the Whitfields' on Friday night—and when the slide projector was brought out about

10:30 PM, he let out a large groan. Charity whisked him off before he could say anything else, so I left with them. I was walking rapidly down the front walk when I realized I was alone and backtracked. Apparently, people linger at the front door. Randy strikes me as perceptive, so I think he noticed, but he seems to find people amusing. I am trying really hard not to commit too many faux pas—but with me, even at home, they are built in.

Guchihi, an older Kikuyu man, is the housekeeper/cook for Charles and Charity. Muthoni is the young woman who helps him. We are getting along chiefly by pantomime since I am not fluent in Kikuyu. One way I am being terribly spoiled is that Muthoni brings me a tea tray at 6:30 AM to wake me up.

There are lots of men and dogs in the large compound. The African dogs all seem enthusiastic about me. They probably can smell my American dog on my clothes. At the Whitfields' house, their Dalmatian puppy was all over me, and Suzanne asked him why he loved me so much. She told him, "You're supposed to love me." The dog didn't answer.

Every day is chock-a-block full. Yesterday, we went to the gliding field, a farm to see the warthogs, the Aberdare Country Club for lunch, the Outspan for racquetball (I walked around), and to the butcher shop for meat. That was an experience. You are very close to the carcasses here. Open doors and windows with no screens, sawdust on the floor, and flies, but not many—we are apparently so high and cool that they are not a serious problem.

31

Public health seems to be generally good, but Randy, an ophthalmologist, said that random testing of the population of a nearby village turned up thirty percent positive for AIDS. A time-bomb is ticking in this part of the world—maybe everywhere.

I am being taken this afternoon to Mountain Lodge to see the wild elephants.

January 24, 1990

I am agog over the beauty of this place. Charity had to go to Nairobi for a couple of days, so I have been staying with Suzanne and Randy Whitfield. Every afternoon after the noise of school (yes, children are the same the world over), we have a peaceful tea on the terrace overlooking Mount Kenya—or rather the base of Mount Kenya, as it is usually wreathed in clouds. The first visiting teacher, Linda Grady, told me how beautiful this place is, but words are inadequate. (I am the second visiting teacher.)

On Sunday, Charles and Charity took me to Mountain Lodge to see the elephants. The elephants decided to be shy, but we saw all sorts of other animals—including the beautiful black-and-white colobus monkey who would have peed on me if I hadn't been swift. It amazed me that elephants live in these thick forests. I thought they lived on the plains. Charles said, "Not the mountain elephants." He also showed me a huge trench that the British forced the Kikuyu to dig all around the base of Mount Kenya to keep in the wildlife. It was slave labor. Charles's father built a false roof in their house in which Charles and his sister hid daily until all the workers in their village had been marched off, and they could come down. It is hard to believe that Kenya has only been independent from the British for twenty-five years. Because I am white, people are a bit standoffish—until they hear my decidedly Southern accent, and they realize I am not British.

On the way back from Mountain Lodge, Charles stopped the car, turned off the lights, and announced, "Darkest Africa."

In many ways, Kenya is like the Ark. The animals have to be preserved here if they are going to exist in the world at all.

I have started my classes. The children are charming, and they keep answering, "Yes" when I ask them if they can understand me. I would find that reassuring, except that they answer, "Yes" to anything I ask them. Mount Kenya Academy is a fine school, but a small one. For the students to change classes, any available faculty member leans out of the staff room window and rings a hand bell—that is, if anyone remembers. The teachers laugh a lot. Many times I have found myself laughing in the staff room when I haven't the foggiest notion why we are laughing. With few exceptions, the teachers work very hard. I am dazzled by how hard everyone works.

January 29, 1990

Suzanne Whitfield's father died suddenly in his sleep. She had just spoken to him on the phone the night before. She is devastated, of course. The Whitfields have now gone to the United States for the funeral.

I have taught lots of children from many different races, but this is the first time I have ever taught Indian children. I am having a terrible time telling the boys from the girls because the Sikh boys don't cut their hair. They wear their hair in buns until they are old enough to wear turbans. When the children have on their P.E. shorts and T-shirts, I frequently can't discern their gender. They are all beautiful.

Yesterday Charles took me to a nearby rural Presbyterian church. The church seems to be flourishing here— overflowing congregation with children wandering in and out of the sanctuary that is open to the air and sunlight. The service was long—over two hours—with lots of men and women at the podium, speaking and taking up the offering. The women wear scarves tied behind their heads in the African manner. Babies are either tied with blankets onto women's backs in uncomfortable-looking positions or held in laps very tenderly. The babies don't seem to be uncomfortable, however, and they must be happy as I never heard one cry. The music is definitely African. The only instrument is a loud drum that beats for hymns and anthems. I discovered that I can *not* listen to a sermon in Kikuyu just as well as I can *not* listen to a sermon in English. The whole service was in Kikuyu. Afterwards, Charles asked me how I knew how to sing hymns in Kikuyu. I said, "I didn't. I just sang them in English."

Last week we went to the Episcopal Church. As I compared them, the Episcopal Church was more prosperous but seemed to lack the vitality of the Presbyterian Church.

Around Nyeri, the landscape is dotted with Catholic and Presbyterian churches. The churches are well past the missionary stage of development—I don't believe they need missionaries any more.

After church, Charles and Charity, friends Helen and Bethwell Kurutu and their daughter Georgina, and I all went jouncing over a terrible road to Charles's trout farm at the base of Mount Kenya. This is an open-air restaurant under trees that looked like American redwoods. The delicious trout were charcoal-grilled and eaten at picnic tables. The setting was absolutely glorious, and we walked around examining gardens and trout ponds. Charles laughed about his workers when we observed his herd of white goats. Although the herd mostly consists of female goats, it never increases or decreases in number.

Then we all bounced on over to the Mount Kenya Safari Club for tea. It is an extremely posh hotel set in the middle of a game park. Apparently, it is frequented by movie stars, as their pictures were all over bulletin boards. The movie stars have good taste—huge windows, green lawns, gorgeous pool, scads of birds visiting the pond, up to and including storks— all with Mount Kenya towering in the distance. We all had on our informal clothes because we had come from the trout farm. We had tea, but then we were asked to leave, because coats and ties are required after 6:00. Charles and Bethwell both laughed, and we all stayed right where we were. We really only drove about a hundred miles round-trip, but it felt like a thousand, because the roads are so bad.

January 31, 1990

The contrast between the haves and the have-nots is staggering, but I am beginning to look beyond the poverty to lifestyle. The people live in dirt-floored huts, yet everyone seems cheerful. I have pondered it a bit, and I realize it is an ancient and communal way of life. Fortunately, in this part of East Africa, agriculture is productive. Everything grows—from oranges through wheat. Corn, called "maize," grows everywhere—even along the edges of roads. There are goats, cows, sheep, chickens all over the place. Donkeys are the beasts of burden, and some of them are badly overworked.

They all have the biblical Sunday off, however. I enjoy seeing the Sabbath freedom of the asses—the four-legged variety. There are many shepherds. I realize that the parts of the Bible that seem archaic to me are timely and current here.

There is a community of squatters' huts close to the beginning of the Mwangis' long driveway. Charles doesn't like it because he is concerned about the health risks; however, he is very sympathetic to the people and explained to me that they have been forced out of the forests by the government. He also explained the way of life that had evolved in the forest with the rotation of crops and planting of trees. That seems ecologically sound. However, the real health risk, I believe, lies in the future for squatters and everybody else—AIDS.

Containing AIDS is hopeless, I think. Dark is so dark here, and when the only lights I have observed at night in the villages are a few kerosene lamps burning here and there among the huts, I realized there is nothing to do after dark except talk and have sex—both ancient pastimes. Unfortunately, there is a deadly disease that is going to hit five or ten years down the road for some of them. My guess is that worrying what is going to hit five or ten years down the road is pretty far down everybody's list of things to worry about.

The climate is as perfect as any on earth, fresh and dewy, twelve hours of daylight and twelve hours of darkness year round. I have never seen stars like this—not only is it darker than the darkest nights I have ever experienced, we are living at a high altitude, and there isn't as much atmosphere between us and the stars.

Labor is so cheap that everyone who is at all prosperous—and some who are not—has help. Charles and Charity have help in the house, in the yard, everywhere. I announced at the dinner table that in Kenya, there was an abundance of labor and that in the United States, we have gadgets. Charles made me get up from the dinner table and go look at the microwave. I told him, "You win. You have both labor *and* gadgets."

People carry your packages to and from the car and even remember your car keys. I am being quite spoiled. It doesn't seem as difficult to work hard at school when the responsibilities for shopping, cooking, and caring for the house are completely lifted off my shoulders. Since I don't even have to worry about answering the telephone, my free time is exactly that—free. Tea is brought to me in the morning before I get up. Usually, nobody else wants breakfast, so I have two boiled eggs and cold toast (in the British manner) quietly by myself while looking out at the roses and drinking more tea. My eggs are great—fresh from hens, to whom I have been introduced, to the table. I don't have to wash or iron. I drop clothes in the hamper, and they magically reappear cleaned and pressed. It's like having a wife.

Shopping for food is a problem. I've gone with Suzanne, and you practically have to kill your own cow. Charity took me to Karatina, one of the largest open-air markets in the world. It was crowded, colorful, and I was the only white person for miles. I had to beat the merchants off with a stick. Everything imaginable was for sale from pineapples through shoes. The pineapple salesman whacked the husk away with a machete and then licked the pineapple—probably to test its quality before giving it to customers. I declined.

I try to open each class that I teach by reading poetry aloud. Myra Livingston is both a poet and an anthologist, and I brought several of her excellent anthologies with me.

Having received the news in a letter that her husband had recently died, I told a class this news while I was reading out of her book about familial situations faced by children, *There Was a Place and Other Poems*. The concern and empathy expressed by the children made me realize what a small world it is—and why I love working with children. We sent her a sympathy card.

February 5, 1990

Everybody is so hospitable. People just call up from Nairobi or wherever and say, "I'm coming for the weekend." Households seem to expand and contract comfortably—or, at least, Charity's does. Charity says that there aren't that many places to stay, so everyone stays with friends. The food is delicious and not very different from my usual food. The food in Kenya is a mixture of British and African. Southern cooking is also a mixture of British and African. There were slabs of white stuff served at school lunch one day with a sort of gravy to go with it. I regarded it with some doubt, but when I tasted it, I realized it was "grits" with more of the moisture cooked out. It's the first time I've ever eaten a slab of grits, but the taste was the same. We also had some kind of green leafy vegetable that was chopped up, seasoned, and cooked. It looked like turnip greens but wasn't. (This is probably where the method of cooking turnip greens and collard greens originated.) The vegetable gardens are glorious—the soil is rich and black. It looks like rich cake. I saw the most beautiful turnip greens on turnips and suggested that they might be cooked as well as the turnips. This suggestion was not greeted with unmitigated enthusiasm. Turnip greens are considered animal fodder.

With not untypical American arrogance, I had felt like I was away from all the "news." Now, however, I'm absorbed in the African news, which was exotic to me in the beginning. Although mostly ignored by the western world, it is very important in the larger scheme of global events. Also, I don't miss U.S. budget problems at all. I have to admit that Daniel arap Moi's government is not an improvement, but I don't think I'd better say anything at all on that subject.

One of the books I brought was called *Out of the Shadows of Night: The Struggle for International Human Rights.* I had received it as a review copy. When I was covering and processing it, I thought, "You'd better read this before you add it to the Mount Kenya Academy collection." I'm glad I did as it had considerable information about Kenya. I whipped it right out of the library and into my book bag to give away safely to Charity. I would *die* if I got Charity in trouble.

An earlier experience, a seemingly innocent one, showed me that getting into trouble is entirely possible. On Fridays, the school has a flag-raising ceremony at which the national anthem is sung. I find it quite interesting and appealing. A different teacher takes part each week by blowing a whistle to make everyone come to attention, and by blowing it again to close the ceremony. Last week, an incompetent whistle-blower was in charge. When she first emitted a weak "cheep," a ripple went through the school children, but they continued the ceremony. When she "cheeped" again, all the children burst into laughter. Charity got really upset. I have never seen her so upset. She said, "We could get into serious trouble with the government for that." An amazing thought to me—but it certainly gave me pause. I am not used to being serious about the government. It is probably salutary to learn how other people cope and feel. The main feeling I get from observing people is "lie low."

The news on television is beyond me, as it is in Kikuyu. When Daniel Moi returned from a week in the United States, I understood that every other word was "American." Everyone is electrified over the possibility of Nelson Mandela getting out of prison. I'll miss U.S. television mightily because of that, as we can't even get the news very well here.

I was amazed when I first talked about Atlanta to Jane Kamau, a gentle first-grade teacher. She said that she could never visit Atlanta because of the child murders. She said that did something to her heart, and she would never want to visit. It did something to my heart too, but I had never pondered the international implications before. And it all happened a decade ago. That "Atlanta" is a bad word to someone on the other side of the world whom I have come to respect is distressing.

I really think that Kenya is wonderful and beautiful. I am now used to seeing women carry things on their heads and babies on their backs, which seems sensible and dignified. As I am roughly their age, I can't get used to seeing old women bent over with big burdens on their backs.

February 12, 1990

Everyone here is ecstatic over the release of Mandela from prison on February 11, 1990. I left early, before the daily papers came, to go gliding and missed the whole thing. I'm sure I will see it tonight, but I regret that I missed seeing it live. My gliding group spent the whole day outdoors and out of touch. Charity and Charles and friends read in the paper that he was going to be released, and they had a party to celebrate. Their daughter Betty even called from England to say that she was watching it on the BBC. The stature of that man. And in this land especially.

If I had to be in the wrong place, I've never been in a better wrong place than the cockpit of a glider. There is very little noise. You can talk to the pilot in a normal voice. The wind blows in your face. It is amazing. Apparently, this is the perfect place for thermal winds, because the land is hot, and the cool air sweeps off the mountains (or something like that). The African countryside from aloft is exquisite. I loved having a bird's-eye view. Going gliding involves lugging chairs, coolers, food, drinks, blankets to sit on, and tarpaulins to set up to provide shade. Then everyone sits around talking, eating, and drinking while waiting one's turn in the one glider. (I can tell from my sunburn today that I should have sat under the tarp a good deal more.) I thoroughly enjoyed it, but it felt familiar to me. I finally realized that it was exactly like lugging stuff to Highland Games, which we did for years when our daughter, Mary Evelyn, participated in Highland dancing. (The Scottish missionaries, who started many of the churches and schools here, even had Charity, as a small child, learning Highland dancing. One of her older brothers, who was a freedom fighter, observed his little sister doing the "Highland Fling." He told her that she didn't even know what she was participating in. Charity's father told her that the most heartbreaking experience of his life was going to collect this brother's body from a pile of bodies of men killed by British soldiers.)

After school today, we went back for tea at the Whitfields' house. Suzanne suggested a walk in the forest. I jumped at the chance. Suzanne retrieved walking sticks and off we went. The forest extends from the river at the bottom of the garden all the way up Mount Kenya. When we got to the river, we took off our shoes and socks, I carefully rolled up my trousers, and we squished through the mud, climbed up the bank, and redressed. We walked various trails with me in a high state of excitement because we could hear the monkeys all around us. We heard a peculiar call, and Suzanne said, "That sounds like a baboon." *A BABOON!* I wasn't hot to trot with a baboon, but I gather one meets what one meets. We had five excited dogs with us (all of whom thoughtfully showered us with river water) so needless to say, all the wildlife for miles around knew we were crashing about in the forest.

Suzanne kept saying, "It's not usually this overgrown." The Dalmatian puppy, who is supposed to be dim-witted, stayed carefully behind Suzanne and in front of me on the whole excursion. Suzanne pointed out elephant poop and elephant damage to trees. *AN ELEPHANT!* Finally she stopped and said, "Uh-oh." That is not what you want to hear in the middle of an African forest.

I said, "What, what?" She pointed to a track in the mud and told me it was a buffalo print. *A BUFFALO!*

She said, "If we meet a buffalo, climb a tree."

I said, "*A TREE?*"

(On hearing this reported later, her husband Randy said, "Kemie, you would have been at the top of a tree before you knew you could climb.")

I was now torn between searching the treetops for monkeys and looking over my shoulder for charging buffalo. Unfortunately, I didn't know to watch my feet for safari ants. When Suzanne stopped laughing, I had my shirt over my head while she picked ants off my back. They pinch twice—the place they decide to pinch and the hand that picks them off. Suzanne said the Maasai use safari ants for sutures. We slogged on. By the time we had climbed over thornbushes and under barbed wire (on our bellies) and arrived back at the river, we both walked right in—socks, shoes, trousers, and all. When we finally arrived back at the house at dark, Suzanne looked at me and massively understated, "Kemie, you look a bit worse for wear."

February 17, 1990

I'm on the balcony of the hotel overlooking the Indian Ocean. With the palm trees, blue ocean, and white sand, it could be Florida—until one notices the monkeys in the palm trees. We are having midterm break at Mount Kenya Academy, and I decided to take a trip by myself to Kenya's coast. I caught the night train from Nairobi to Mombasa. I haven't spent the night on a train since childhood. The porter who made up my bed was extremely solicitous, and when I asked him how to lock the door, he wanted to know if I was scared. I said, "No, I just want to know how to lock the door."

After dinner, I locked the door, put on my nightgown, and leaned out the window for a long time. The sheer expansiveness of Africa is hard to absorb. The land is so dark, and the stars are so bright. The only lights to be seen anywhere are the lights of the train when it enters a curve. The air is cool and fresh. (I wasn't the only person leaning out. A head poked out of the next window and jumped when I said, "Hello.")

Mombasa is hot as hell and twice as dirty. When daylight came a couple of hours before we arrived, I saw many collections of round, mud-walled, thatched huts. They looked like part of the landscape, but children emerged from the huts in sparkling white shirts and colorful school uniforms. The houses are completely biodegradable. I saw them in all stages of collapsing back into the land. A tin roof is obviously desirable, and the huts changed from round to square to

45

accommodate the large square pieces of tin. What fits into a rural landscape, however, becomes squalor when crowded into slums. I will never take running water for granted again. No words or pictures can convey the enormous number of people lugging large plastic water containers back and forth.

Some scenes were so appalling that they are burned onto my retinas. Pitifully poor people were picking through the large and smoking Mombasa dump. Another was seeing the Mombasa Blood Bank in a slum with a "Blood Donors Welcome" sign. If any poor soul needs a blood transfusion, it is obviously a "pick your poison" decision. (I repeat that I think few Kenyans have much choice about what will or will not happen five or ten years down the road. Tomorrow is a big enough worry.)

Mombasa's "old town" may have been equally dirty, but at least it was dirty with character—narrow streets and balconies leaning over streets. The stone quay at the old harbor made me sick, literally, because it was where the slave ships were loaded. The old Portuguese "Fort Jesus" was not the site of much happiness either. Those Portuguese were hellions. I walked into a Hindu temple off of a dirty street, and it was cool, clean, and quiet. The interesting paintings around the walls were stylized, flat, opaque, and decorated with gold. One wall had English translations under the pictures. I was padding around barefoot reading these and was quite startled by the one that read, "No pain, no gain."

I have ambivalent feelings about staying in a luxury hotel on the beach after seeing such poverty. I didn't know what to do, so I ended up doing nothing and staring at the ocean. I did have one happy experience in town. I went to a wood-carving cooperative. Someone gathered a lot of wood-carvers together, to build low, thatched-roof, open-air huts. The floors were dirt but aromatic from all the wood shavings. It was a sort of wood-carving factory, although the wood-carvers are artisans. I felt foolish walking around looking at wood-carvers, but since I am a tourist, I went ahead and peered.

I have enjoyed watching the beautiful, little redheaded yellow weaver birds in the tall reeds by my open-air breakfast table. Their gourd-shaped, hanging nests obviously require a lot of upkeep, and they all twitter and work diligently at housekeeping first thing every morning. One chap worked and worked unsuccessfully to break off a long stem, and another brought a leaf and nibbled it to death to get at the vein with which to weave. One had pulled down two flowery branches on a nearby bush and had woven a nest at the intersection. How do you suppose he held the branches down long enough to weave? Some are more diligent than others, and all are more diligent than me.

February 24, 1990

Suzanne Whitfield and I are sitting on somebody's veranda (somebody who is conveniently out of town), looking south over Lake Naivasha to the Mau Escarpment on the other side of the Rift Valley—the cradle of humanity. To the left of us, there is a veil of rain with lightning flashing and the sun shining through holes in the clouds. Also to the left, the distant hills are clear and blue. Suzanne's daughter Louisa goes to a British boarding school here called Pembroke. The kids are going sailing on Lake Naivasha tomorrow, and I was lucky enough to be invited along for the ride. We went north to cross the Aberdare Mountains and the equator at 8,000 feet. Then we went south on the other side of the Aberdares down into the beautiful Rift Valley. The mountains are green with trees and golden with grass. The Kenyans are extremely fond of cows, sheep, and goats, and the countryside is crawling with them. They all seem to live quite peacefully with herds of zebra. I almost fell out of the Land Rover when I saw my first herd of zebra. We saw many—each herd closer to the road than the last until we stopped, and they all lifted their heads and looked alertly at us. However, they seem to be quite used to people. This whole experience reminds me of traveling back in time.

At home, the mail is no longer important. It is all junk mail. Here the mail functions like it used to at home. I get excited when I receive a letter, and so does everyone else. Letters are bright spots for all and sundry.

Books are also highly cherished here. Everyone seems to love and appreciate them. There are no current magazines floating around, very few people have television, and for those that do, the reception is lousy. The good side of this is that it warms my heart to see books valued. The dark side is heartbreaking. Yesterday, I visited a school sponsored by the Presbyterian Church with seven hundred children and not one book. (One can hardly aspire to be the "book teacher" in Kenya if there are no books.) The teaching tools consist of the front wall of the classrooms painted black—and chalk. The children sit on benches. There are no panes in the windows; the floors are dirt. There is a row of battered tin outhouses over drop holes for toilets. Yet, the school is neat and orderly, and the children seem happy. The kitchen is a shed with a big pot bubbling over a wood fire in the middle of the floor. The cooks were amused by my coughing and hacking, and they laughed over my suggestion that they needed a chimney.

The children found me hilarious. I sounded funny, and I definitely looked funny. The children stood politely whenever I entered a classroom and grinned at me, but I heard waves of laughter after I left. (It hurts me to think of all the books at home. There must be some way to get them here.) I will give this school half of the books purchased with the grant from the Susan B. Russell Foundation. I was so careful to be politically correct with the books I brought. I brought picture books featuring African animals; I brought books set in Africa; I brought books featuring black children. The students at Mount Kenya Academy have asked me, "Don't you have any more Hardy Boys books? Don't you have any more Baby-Sitters Club books?" They want all the type books that I left at home. I will ask John to pack up all those books and air freight them to me.

February 26, 1990

Yesterday, I went with Suzanne to Lake Naivasha to watch Louisa go sailing with the Pembroke kids before we took Louisa back to Pembroke. This event took place on an island in the lake that we reached by a muddy causeway that is usually under water. As we bumped across, the ducks, the coots, the pelicans, and other water birds flew away from in front of us in droves. Even the starlings in Kenya are breathtaking—green backs, red breasts, white rumps, shining feathers. There was a herd of waterbucks on the island. Bea, a little girl from England who is at Pembroke for a term, and I crept over close to observe them.

When we left, we drove some of the parents to the local airstrip—using the term loosely. We looked back. A storm had come and gone over us, and the sun was shining on the surface of the lake. We were at a lower elevation than the lake, and it was as if there was a shining line all above the horizon. It seemed to be in the sky. I maintain that light and space are natural antidepressants, and Kenya has an abundance of both.

We were driving back to Pembroke with Louisa squeezed in the front seat of the Land Rover between Suzanne and me. As we got closer to school Louisa said, "I always get a stomach-ache when I reach Gilgil (pronounced 'Gilly-Gilly,') I don't know why." She was having "Leaving-Suzanne-Sickness," poor thing. I went inside the school to see Louisa's bed, and I heard crying in the bathroom. I went to investigate and discovered Bea crying. I put my arms around her, and she leaned against me, sobbing with homesickness. It's been a long time since I've felt a child cry that hard; she was absolutely shuddering by the time the "storm" of crying was over. She goes home at the end of March, so obviously we are not all equally delighted with Kenya. It makes me wonder about Pembroke. The rooms are light and airy with six little beds in each room. The children looked charming in their gray wool pants, skirts, and sweaters, but neither of the two inmates that I knew well were charmed.

I have, however, discovered a big flaw in falling in love with a faraway place and faraway people. When you're there, you have loved ones on the other side of the world—and vice versa. There seems to be no solution. And I have fallen in love with these people. Charles is witty and amazingly sanguine at having a live-in guest. Charity is a kind and brilliant educator. And I love Suzanne and Louisa—and on and on.

Another "Charity," Mrs. Ngunjiri, took me to see two schools out in the boondocks, and then she took some faculty members from the second school and me to her house for lunch. It was a small, tidy house with spotless white covers on the sofa and chairs in the main room. There was a basin of warm water with soap and a towel to wash our hands before we served ourselves the food. The honored guest got to use the water first. The hostess used it last. The doors were open to the fresh air, and some children and a hen peeped in.

March 3, 1990

My husband John and daughter Mary Evelyn get here at 11:00 PM on March 31. I can't wait to see them. I decided to hire a driver for our safari. Not only do they drive on the wrong side of the road here (or maybe *we* drive on the wrong side of the road), they use clutches and gears. John and I haven't shifted gears since adolescence. Many Kenyans also drive like maniacs, and their roads are terrible. I was told that they kill forty times as many people in traffic accidents per population as we do in the United States, and we're no slouches in the killing department. It's absolute carnage, and I wouldn't have a moment's peace if John was driving with our daughter in the car—let alone, me. Life is too precious and time is too short. I-95 is a little country drive compared to this. The roads in Kenya are swarming with "matatus." They are small private vans that make more money the more people they pack in, and the faster they go.

Last night, we went to eat with Charity's sister Wanjiru, her husband Theo Sababady, and their son Thomas of "cute little fat boy" fame. When we arrived, Charles said, "I see The Minister is here." I took off my shoes and went bumbling in thinking that the preacher was also dining. It was not the preacher but a government "Minister," a huge, intimidating man who visits Charles from time to time, probably because Charles laughs and jokes with him, and my guess is that few people do.

When I walked into the living room, there he was. I reluctantly shook his hand. I then went into my "Who-me?-I-know-nothing" mode, and I didn't say a word all evening except to the Sababadys' little son, Thomas. To my amusement, Thomas, who was oblivious to the supreme importance of their guest, made an absolute nuisance of himself all evening. When The Minister wanted Thomas to quiet down so he could pontificate, Thomas would not. He actually told Thomas once to be quiet to no avail. Unlike the effect he must normally have on people, Thomas paid absolutely no attention to him.

During the course of the evening, The Minister referred to Charles as "my best friend." (Yeah—right. I've got news for him. Charles can laugh and joke and reveal nothing.) Later, when I mentioned to Charles that The Minister complained that his wife doesn't agree with his politics, he said, "That's because his wife is straight, and he's like a corkscrew."

Today, I went with Charity to a party. It was the eightieth birthday of an old British colonialist, Sylvia Richardson. The BBC had made a documentary about her called *My African Farm*—which the British hated, and the French loved. It won some kind of French award—probably because it exposed the worst side of British colonial attitudes. Charles and Charity were the token African guests. The many other Africans there were serving the refreshments. All over the garden there were tents with tablecloth-covered tables spread with food and flowers. The guests were British from all over Kenya.

Many had flown in to the local airstrip. For a moment, it was the remnants of a way of life that doesn't exist any more.

I met an antique dealer who had sold his business and moved to Kenya. He told me that he couldn't make it in Kenya because of all the money "under the table," so he was moving to Mexico. He said he liked "the style of life" in Kenya and Mexico. He said it was available in the U.S. but was too expensive. What he probably meant is that he liked servants. Charming fellow.

Some people were nice to Charity, but she was patronized a lot. (I was not patronized, because I was totally invisible.) Charity is very astute and picks up on vibes. She finally looked at me and said, "I'm not doing this again. This is *my* country." Charles picks up on vibes too, I think, but he seems to just enjoy the free-flowing liquids and thinks the people are funny.

One elderly white man came over and started talking to us as we were getting ready to leave. He was very pleasant, but he finally said that he had to get a glass of water because he couldn't drink any more wine. Charity asked, "Why not?"

He said, "I've got a long way to drive, and I have to be sober to deal with the matatus."

Then he added, "But you wouldn't know about that."

Charity looked baffled and said, "Why wouldn't I know about matatus?"

He said, "Because you're not out on the roads like I am."

Charity looked at me and said, "Come on, Kemie. Let's walk back to my shamba!"

March 9, 1990

The faculty is so busy and hardworking that they are exhausting to try to emulate. This includes Suzanne Whitfield, Mrs. Dillard (a talented music teacher who is the wife of a Baptist missionary), and Rebecca Njogu (a bright young teacher with two clever boys in school here). Her husband was tragically killed in Nairobi, leaving her a widow to raise their two sons. Among others, there are also two slender and nice young men from Uganda on the faculty, Mr. Stanley and Mr. Jerome. Charles humorously calls both of them "The Other One."

One young man from Sweden is also a visiting teacher. He arrived with family in tow. He frequently accompanies the singing in assembly with his guitar. In Sweden, I believe it is customary when people go swimming to dress and undress at the beach. People politely look away. The Kenyans I have met, however, are modest and wouldn't dream of undressing in public. Nevertheless, the teacher's wife followed the Swedish custom by undressing and putting on her bathing suit by the side of the school's lovely blue swimming pool. This caused a sensation among the students who had never seen anyone undress in public—let alone a white woman. Much amazement, accompanied by giggles and whispers and children who didn't politely look away, ensued until Charity got wind of the situation and put a stop to it.

Charity and Charles left for Nairobi yesterday morning. They were—among other errands—going to pick up my order from Permabound, a book company. I will never order from them again as I should have received my order weeks before I left the U.S. I'm now completely wedded to the Bound-to-Stay-Bound book company with their almost indestructible books, lovely covers, and great customer service. I have spent the entire term teaching without the Permabound books that I had planned to use. Thanks to them, I have also spent the whole term answering, "It's in the box that is coming."

Student question: "Have you got a picture of Cerberus?"

Answer: "It's in the box that is coming."

When Charity and Charles couldn't get back from Nairobi, I had the house and staff, Guchihi and Muthoni, to myself. I asked them to come watch a video with me. Guchihi is a stout, bald, older man, and Muthoni is a young woman. They sat on the rug, and we watched *Eleni*. Here in Africa was a Kikuyu-speaking elderly man watching a Greek movie in English. Muthoni, who speaks English, translated into Kikuyu occasionally, but I do wonder what he made of it. Since it was mostly rural Greek countryside with the women doing hard labor, he could probably understand it. They are both kind, nice people.

AIDS is coming down the pike toward all of these kind, nice Africans—and toward those who are neither. The Africans that I know don't talk about it. It may be respectability that causes a reluctance to talk about sex, I don't know. When I was speaking at a faculty meeting at one of the government schools, someone asked me about problems in America. I answered that probably our worst social problems are guns, drugs, and AIDS. They seemed shocked that I talked about AIDS aloud. It is a growing problem here, although it has yet to strike in full force. The rumor mill conveys that there are whole villages in Uganda where all of the babies and middle generation have perished, leaving only the old people to take care of the children. Like all rumors, it probably contains a kernel of truth.

March 20, 1990

Last Friday night, Suzanne was driving me home in the Land Rover down Charity's long driveway, and I started laughing. Suzanne wanted to know why I was laughing, but I could hardly answer, I was so tickled. She started laughing too. I said, "Look at us."

We were windblown, dirty, exhausted, and disheveled—our usual condition after any excursion together. We wear each other out and wind up in a state of collapse. I told Suzanne that was part of her charm. In this instance, we had just chaperoned the entire class of Standard Seven (ten girls, eighteen boys) on an overnight trip to Nairobi. We had all of the girls in the Land Rover with us, and we had managed to think up a few extra things to do with the girls. Suzanne is a wonderful friend, but I don't think we should grow old together. At this rate, we will both be old by Christmas.

I have never thought of myself as particularly fastidious—no one who works with children can keep up that pretense—

57

but I guess I was. I have made my peace with dirt. If you are going to get upset about a little dirt, don't come to Africa. Charity fights an endless battle keeping her house and her school up to her high standards of cleanliness, but most people either can't or don't. African women wear scarves around their heads. I thought it was just their style, but it helps to keep the dust out of their hair. While affluent Africans like the Mwangis have plenty of hot water, for most people, hot water is precious and is measured by the teacup full. There is little hot water for bathing. I used to notice body odor—then I noticed it, but didn't mind it—now I don't even notice it. I'm sure they are returning the favor.

So much here tickles me. People are far more alike than they are different. The same phenomenon calls forth different expressions. Today it was raining while the sun was shining. I said, "The devil is beating his wife."

Charity laughed and said, "The hyenas are getting married." Nuances and expressions go on and on. We say, "uh-huh," with our mouths closed during conversations to show that we are listening to what is being said. The Kikuyu say, "Eh," with their mouth open to convey the same thing. I hear it everywhere and may take it up. The other day, Charity said, "It's like the boy who cried, 'Hyena.'"

When the time came to say goodbye to my students, I took charge of the assembly. We sang songs and put on a play featuring Greek Mythology (one of their favorite subjects and mine). For a finale, I led them in singing "Lord of the Dance," and everyone joined in singing the chorus repeatedly as we joined hands, and I led them down to make a huge singing circle around the entire playground.

Yes, I am aware that the song is from my culture (or rather from the "Shaker" culture). I am also aware that fun is universal.

"'Dance then wherever you may be,
I am the Lord of the Dance,' said He,
'And I'll lead you all wherever you may be,
I'll lead you all in the Dance,' said He."

Children holding water bottles filled with water collected from a nearby stream (Photograph by Abi Joy Nix)

CHAPTER TWO
1992

January 26, 1992

My son Johnny and I have arrived and moved into one of the Outspan Hotel's three cottages. Charles, Charity, their daughter Betty, and her friend came to dinner here. We are staying at the Outspan until Betty returns to England next weekend. Our cottage has two bedrooms, a sitting room with a fireplace, and a bathroom. The Outspan is a wonderful, old British Empire hotel in Nyeri with dark timbering, white plaster, lots of chintz, and sweeping lawns with flowers galore. You can guess that Johnny and I are roughing it. Last night, the person who was supposed to meet us at the airport didn't. That wasn't pleasant at 1:00 in the morning, and I had foolishly neglected to find out which hotel had our reservations. I guessed correctly, however, so we took a taxi and finally arrived at the Norfolk Hotel in Nairobi.

I'm in my nightgown and robe since my electric blanket is not with me—as I mentioned, roughing it. We left in winter and arrived in summer. My quick impression, after two years: Kenya seems more prosperous. The hundred miles from Nyeri was a nightmare when I left—bone-shattering potholes the complete way. Now the entire hundred miles has been repaved. The small, crowded truck-like vans, matatus, have been replaced with large, white, new, clean vans. I was impressed. The few matatus were oddities that I pointed out to Johnny.

The most amazing thing of all is that on the way to Nyeri I only saw one woman with a baby on her back. In 1990, it seemed as if every walking woman had a baby on her back. Birth control has obviously swept the country. That is a good thing for the women. I had been told by Charles on my first visit that Kenya had the highest birthrate in the world.

January 29, 1992

I'm lying in my bed with a blazing fire across the room. Johnny is in the next room packing his backpack to climb Mount Kenya. He suddenly decided to go tomorrow, so he walked into Nyeri to get his food. He told me that he is excited. He plans to walk from school to base camp at Naro Moru River Lodge tomorrow. Then he plans to stay at the youth hostel overnight, where he hopes to meet up with some other climbers. I figure he is acclimated after three or four days at this altitude. I don't blame him for being excited as climbing Mount Kenya is the adventure of a lifetime.

Planning is fun to me. All Johnny has to do is make the slightest suggestion, and my mind is off and running. I got so carried away with plans that I pulled myself up short and told Johnny I was always full of suggestions. He looked at me tolerantly and said, "I know—but I don't mind."

February 1, 1992

Mount Kenya Academy now has a full-fledged school bus, which picks us up at the Outspan every morning. Johnny caused a small sensation when he climbed aboard this morning in all of his mountain-climbing gear. Our next stop was the nursery school, where we drop off some tiny children and pick up others, including Jennifer Ide, who is no longer tiny. I also taught Jennifer, who was in Johnny's class at Westminster. She is spending a year teaching at Mount Kenya Academy. She is doing a wonderful job and is flourishing. Life is beyond amazing. If anyone had ever told me that someday I would be jouncing down a road with Jennifer and Johnny on a school bus in Africa, I *never* would have believed them.

School is wonderful. I have taught most of these children, and I am fond of them, and they seem to be fond of me. Everybody laughs at my least little sally. On my 1990 visit, I forgot to bring any stockings, so I spent an entire term teaching in trousers with red socks. Charles called me, "The American Red Socks." In order for the children to recognize me when I went around to say hello to all the classes, I turned around to show them my bun and velvet hair ribbon. I lifted up my trouser leg to show them my red socks. One of the children in Standard Four—who was in Standard Two on my last stint—held up her hand. When I called on her, she tactfully said that, yes, it was me, "But you used to look a lot younger."

More memorable than clothing, however, was my performance in the library in front of the entire Standard Six. While they were being taught by Jennifer, I was washing shelves, preparing them for new books. I informed the students to listen to the lesson and just to consider me invisible. I then scrubbed a top shelf and stepped backwards off the chair up to my knee in a bucket of soapy water.

Jennifer cheerfully informed me that the students would never forget it. She told me that she still remembers when one of her teachers stepped in a trash can. The next morning on the school bus, I asked the children in the row behind me if they had heard that I had stepped in a bucket of water. They brightened right up and gleefully conceded that they had. Indeed, there was no one on the packed school bus who hadn't heard.

February 5, 1992

After Johnny returned from climbing Mount Kenya, he taught a few classes in the library on how to use calculators. He is loud, and I could hear him talking and laughing when I was in the staff room. He will also spend the night with Mrs. Ngunjiri, the Standard Two teacher. They will visit Muruguru Primary School in the morning and Marua in the afternoon. They might kill a goat.

I haven't started teaching a regular schedule yet, though I have met with all the older classes. We are still processing books. We are easily going to have more than four hundred new books. I plan to do most of my running around while Johnny is here and will settle into a routine after he leaves. We get along famously as he regards me with lofty, amused tolerance, and I thrive in such a benign atmosphere.

I am lolling about at the Outspan after a wakeful night at Treetops peering at the animals. Treetops was fun. I thought it was a complete lark when the "great-white-hunter" type unslung his rifle, and we skulked from shelter to shelter making our way to the hotel—until we came out from behind one shelter to observe three Cape buffalo nearby eyeing us suspiciously. We—including a group of British bird-watchers, one of my favorite "types"—saw lions and a rhino and innumerable small birds and animals. I enjoyed the bush baby who chased the civet off the porch rail and the baboon mother of twins who sat as patiently as any human mother while her twins played and played and played on a fallen dead tree. I particularly liked the sleeping wood ducks floating around the edges of the water hole who woke up to a man when the white-tailed mongoose came down to drink.

The fauna is enjoyable here—both domestic and wild. It amuses me to see cows galumphing across the playground, goats wandering around in the roads, not to mention sheep and chickens everywhere. Yesterday, we were driving down Charity's long, grassy driveway on our way home from school and encountered three donkeys on the loose. As we approached, they kicked up their heels and galloped away. One of them was young and obviously enjoying himself. I really like Sundays, because the donkeys are all loose on the Sabbath. Almost everyone obeys the commandment, "Neither thy ox nor thy ass..."

February 15, 1992

Last weekend, Suzanne, Johnny, Jennifer, and I went horseback riding, walking in the forest, and camping in Samburu. I hadn't been on a horse since I was twelve. I figured the best thing to do was take the bull by the horns, so to speak, so I dashed ahead and asked the groom which was the gentlest horse. I was mounted by the time the others strolled up. The English saddle had no pommel to hold onto, of course, but I managed until my horse decided to trot. It wasn't until we returned and I slid off the horse that I learned my horse had the descriptive name, "Peppercorn." Johnny's horse was named, "Johnny."

When we arrived back at the Whitfields', we had tea on the terrace before we went for a walk in the forest. We crossed the Nairobi River, a mere mountain stream on that day. (When Mary Evelyn was here in 1990, she wanted to walk in the forest, but the Nairobi River was too swollen for us to get across.) I consider walking in the forest an adventure. Although we never do meet anything, the potential for meeting something is always there. Even the dogs walk around looking up into the trees. There is elephant poop all over the place, but Suzanne said that the elephants don't come down to drink until evening. Since it was about five minutes until that vague time, I did not find this information reassuring. When we heard what sounded like a trumpet behind us, Johnny and Jennifer were eager to go back and look. Suzanne and I hastily changed course and headed back across the river with two disappointed elephant hunters trailing behind us.

The next day, Johnny, Jennifer, Suzanne, and I traveled north to a tented camp in the middle of Samburu District by the edge of a crocodile-infested river. Our tents were large and airy (with beds, not cots) with porches on the front. I sat overlooking the slow, muddy river. It was still the dry season in an already drought-stricken area. When we walked back from dinner, I looked across the river at the tall thorn trees. With narrow fern-like leaves, they looked like black lace against the gray sky. Throughout the lace were randomly sprinkled baboon-shaped knots. The next morning I watched the knots from my bed. They stirred, stretched, and walked down the branches and trunks—all except one lazy slug-a-bed like me.

I also enjoyed watching the black-faced vervet monkeys that are the squirrels of Samburu. They scamper across the ground and through the trees just like the squirrels at home, and they seem every bit as common. They are obviously very bright, as some monkeys sat on the railing close to us at teatime, creating a diversion with Suzanne and Jennifer while another monkey snuck up behind them and snatched their rolls. A monkey's life doesn't appear to be very strenuous. The mothers lolled about grooming each other on sunlit branches while their youngsters played. Even the tiniest baby played with the larger monkeys. It got stepped on frequently without any obvious ill effects. I don't imagine that vervet children weigh very much. The baby jumped around as lightly as thistledown.

What I don't understand is why some silhouettes appeal aesthetically to the human eye, like the outline of a baby monkey, while the outline of a baboon does not. Or the delicate outline of a gazelle as opposed to the slumped lines of a hyena. Maybe it is an inborn instinct in humans to avoid predators.

February 19, 1992

Johnny and I took a long weekend and flew to the Masai Mara in the south bordering Tanzania. We also stayed in a tented camp there and took long game drives. We took a nature walk that I enjoyed as much as the game drives. The plains really are incredible, teeming with life, yet strewn with the bones of the dead. The animals and people are elegant. I am filled with admiration for the Maasai women who build houses out of sticks and cow dung. I'm sure I couldn't build anything out of cow dung.

We were invited into a hut and stooped and went in and tried not to touch the walls. In an already small hut, one side was partitioned off for the goats and the other for the people. There were two cowhide-covered platforms, one for the men and one for the women, with a small fireplace in between. There was no outlet for the smoke, but I was told that the smoke and the goat urine keep down the mosquitoes. The cow dung is at hand, so to speak, as the cows spend the night in the central round area, ringed by the huts and a high thorny hedge—contributed by the men.

In the rainy season, which is just beginning, the women spend lots of time on the roof applying fresh cow dung. I was told the government has sent hut builders from the Luo tribe to teach the Maasai how to thatch a roof. A smattering of huts over a wide area had thatched roofs—so, apparently, thatched roofs are slowly spreading. They also have a dispensary for medicines for a large area, and the children have schools. On the whole, however, the Maasai continue to live their ancient nomadic life that is being severely stressed by the modern world. (The word is spelled "Maasai" when referring to the tall, elegant people dressed in red scattered across the landscape.) They have their people, their bright robes, their ornaments, their goats and cows, and a gorgeous landscape filled with predators—not to mention lots and lots of cow dung. There were other tourists besides Johnny and me who also stopped by the village. Here were the Maasai women and children supposedly singing a "Welcome" song—with the tourists on the other side in their safari clothes snapping pictures. (Jennifer Ide has dubbed them the "Khaki People," which I think is quite apt.) Talk about two worlds colliding. I have to admit that the slim, straight, red-robed Maasai looked better than the dumpy, disheveled Khaki People. Although I didn't have on safari clothes, you can guess to which group I belonged.

Later our driver was stopped by a Maasai herdsman so Johnny and I could see the huge crocodiles. I didn't look at the herdsman beyond a quick glance, because I didn't want to appear disrespectful. Another quick glance told me that he was studying me with obvious amusement.

It is mind-boggling to think of all the animals that live off of grass...or the grass eaters.

The whole area is awash in grass eaters, and the grass is strewn with their bones. I know of no other place where life and death are so visibly interwoven. Some of the grass eaters are more intelligent than others. The zebra cover the plains in the daytime and climb up among the rocks at night, because the lions can't chase them among the rocks. Johnny and I went on a dawn game drive and met the zebras walking single file down the road from the hills. We were told that the wildebeests will just stand there watching the lions eating their relatives.

We particularly enjoyed watching the young elephants at play. They have a delightful game that could be called "klonking heads." One or the other of two backs up, shuffles its feet, and then runs head on into the other. They obviously consider it great fun when both youngsters manage to back up at the same time and get more momentum into the KLONK.

We also saw a week-old tiny elephant. He was experimenting with his wonderful trunk, twirling it around and grasping air, copying his mother's grass-eating movements. He kept lifting his feet and shaking them. I could only suppose that the grass tickled. On the dawn drive, we also saw a lion family reunion. The mother and father came back from a night of hunting. The mother sat on a hillock and called. Two cubs came out of a drainpipe under the road and ran to her. They all greeted each other most affectionately.

I am not sure how much fun I will have next week, but Johnny wants me to go, so I am going. We are planning to walk across the Aberdares. We leave on Wednesday morning, go to one of the gates to pick up a guard with a gun, and then drive to another gate to set out walking across the high ridge of the Aberdares. We are due to be picked up Saturday by Randy if we don't get "et" by lions. Suzanne mentioned last night that the Aberdares had been closed for years because of the lions. I asked, "What happened to the lions?"

Suzanne assured me, "They shot them."

Oh, well, in that case, if Suzanne says so...

February 29, 1992

We survived the Aberdares. Suzanne, who is a passionate camper, said it was the hardest camping trip she has ever been on. Guess who was a complete greenhorn? This trek turned into an Atlanta trek as, with wise foresight, Charity declined to go. "We" consisted of Robin Richards, who is visiting Kenya, Jennifer Ide, Johnny, Suzanne, me, and our armed guide, Waigwa (pronounced "Y-g wa").

I am not terribly fond of activities in which there is no door marked "Exit." When we entered the "high gate of the Aberdares" at ten thousand feet, the exit was approximately twenty-five miles away—hiking. My heart was pounding so terribly the first day, probably caused by a combination of altitude and lack of fitness on my part, that I abandoned my backpack. I thought I was going to have to be carried out feet first. Johnny said he would go back for it, but Waigwa quickly produced it. After that, Suzanne divided up my stuff, with Johnny carrying most of it, and I just had a day pack. Since everyone else was carrying the tents and food, I really wimped out on them. Although I found that I could carry a little more each day, they should have abandoned me to be "et."

We hiked up hill and down dale, through the forest, through waist-high grass, across streams, and through bamboo—lots and lots of bamboo. Waigwa would shush us whenever he thought there might be animals around. I wasn't too concerned when he was using his rifle as a walking stick, but whenever he carried it in a "ready" position, I got a little more alert. Apparently, there are more animals at lower altitudes, as we had to be much quieter on Friday. We were walking across a meadow when Waigwa pointed to some mashed grass and informed us that was where the lions liked to sleep. (Lions were not native to the Aberdares and were introduced somehow.) A little further down as we were walking across a large expanse, Waigwa told us that the rhino liked this area. Since we walked in single file, and I was a little slower than the others, I usually walked at the back and Johnny walked behind me (to take care of me, I suppose). At the word "rhino" I turned and looked back at Johnny, and his whole face lit up. He said, "Wouldn't it all be worth it if we saw a rhino?" By this time, I knew I could keep up and was enjoying myself immensely.

To add a little more excitement to the occasion, Jennifer came running back saying, "Get back, get back, *RHINO!*"

Ever alert in an emergency, I stood still looking around pondering, "Get back, *WHERE?*"

Waigwa was an incredible guide. I have always been passionately fond of the movie *Dersu Uzala* about the Mongolian hunter who served as a guide to Russian soldiers. Well, now I know a Dersu of my own. Waigwa had lived in the forest for five years when he was very young. That meant he was a freedom fighter, which explains why he knew it so well. (There can't be many of them left.) He once pointed to bamboo leaves on brown mud in the bamboo thickets and told us that the freedom fighters liked the bamboo leaves because they could walk without leaving footprints, and the British soldiers couldn't walk without making noise.

He knew all about the animals, the forest, the trails. Twice I noticed that he changed direction when he heard bird calls in the distance. I wondered if he was leading us away from animals. It rained a couple of nights, but he not only built fires in the rain, he kept them going all night. He told us that the animals smell the smoke and know "The Boss" is in the forest. On Thursday, we ended up camping in a small meadow. This location didn't entirely please Waigwa because we were camping on the pathway of the animals to the river. In the morning, he showed us broken branches that he had placed across the path to tell the animals that we were there. It seemed a funny way to keep elephants away, but it worked. (It was probably Waigwa's snoring that really kept the elephants away. It was of the decibel level of a jet taking off, and I don't know how Johnny, who stayed in the tent with him nightly, got any sleep at all.)

My friend Charlotte Kelley accuses me of making what she has dubbed, "statements." If anyone asks me anything, I will answer whether I know the answer or not. Charlotte has resolved this by asking me, "Kemie, do you really *know* that or are you just making a statement?" She needs to meet Suzanne.

I was trying not to drink unfiltered or unboiled water, but I was thirsty. I was peering dubiously at a stream that the elephants had muddied. Suzanne was encouraging me to go ahead and drink when I protested that the elephants had been here. In the granddaddy of all statements, Suzanne said, "Elephants don't have germs…(pause)…they're *VEGETARIANS!*"

We never met a single animal. On our last night, however, we had a large campfire, and I was sitting on the far side with my back to a log when we heard a peculiar coughing noise. Waigwa told us that the leopard had made a kill and was calling his wife to come and eat. I hastily got up and went to sit by Waigwa, who was sitting under a tree. Since he was wearing camouflage, all I could see of him was his grin.

Later that night as I was trying to settle myself in my sleeping bag on the pebbles and hard ground, I was wondering what in the world I was doing in a sleeping bag on a mountain in Africa. Then Jennifer snuggled down in her sleeping bag saying, "You can't help but be happy when you're in a sleeping bag!"

When we finally walked out of the forest and found Randy and the Land Rover waiting for us, Suzanne cried, "I don't want it to be over." I didn't want it to be over either. The guard at The Ark gate was amazed to hear we had walked across the Aberdares. He peered at me and boggled, "Even the Old Mama?"

March 14, 1992

The political situation in Kenya is grim. Kenya is presently controlled by one political party, KANU, with Daniel arap Moi as president. He is being forced to give ground inch by reluctant inch. Last year, the "multiparty system" was legalized, and there are now several opposition parties, with the two strongest being the Forum for the Restoration of Democracy (FORD) and the Democratic Party (DP). Charles supports DP, and he gave Johnny a DP membership card. Before Johnny went to the airport, I had a sinking feeling about him having both his armed services identification card and a DP card in his wallet. Just to be on the safe side, I cleared both out of his wallet, because I didn't want him to be arrested as a spy.

Many people who fought for the multiparty system are still in jail despite the fact that what they fought for is now legal. These political prisoners have friends in low places—their mothers. A few days ago, these mothers went on a hunger strike in a public park in Nairobi. The government sent in the police to beat them, disperse them, and ferry them back to their respective homes. The defenseless women stripped naked to show their outrage. (I was reading this in the newspaper in the staff room with shock. Apparently, stripping naked is the last and most effective weapon for women. For instance, if a son or daughter is determined to do something that his or her mother is adamantly and ferociously opposed to, she begins to strip. She usually wins the argument at this dire junction.) While westerners might not understand why the mothers stripped, the Africans understood instantly. It was explained to me by Mr. Stanley in the staff room. (Stanley is one of the two young teachers that Charles always humorously refers to as "The Other One.")

The mothers were arrested and the police took them back to their homes all over the country. By now, the government had outraged just about everyone. The mothers, of course, promptly rushed back to the park and chained themselves together so that they couldn't be dispersed. Pictures of weakened mothers in chains were very moving. Forced by the police to leave the park, the mothers are now starving themselves in the basement of All Saints Cathedral. As many of them have been on a hunger strike for two weeks, some of them are beginning to collapse.

At the time of this letter, Professor Wangari Maathai, who is politically active in opposition to the present government and has been arrested more than once, is working with the mothers. A few days ago, she was thoroughly beaten, hospitalized, and has emerged more determined than ever. She is a woman of great courage who, among other achievements, stopped a four-story statue of Moi from being placed in the park. She also started the Green Belt Movement, which is spreading.

Elections are slated before the end of the year—but no one knows when. The tension is increasing. Violence is also increasing with everyone blaming each other. KANU is busily pointing at the violence, which everyone believes they have instigated, saying, "This proves Kenyans are not mature enough for a multiparty system. It will just lead to tribal warfare." They don't seem to perceive the irony of using the exact same argument that the British used during independence when they didn't want to cease governing.

Tourism is way down. Tourists have been attacked in Masai Mara and at Buffalo Springs in Samburu where our group swam in the desert springs. The Outspan Hotel in Nyeri said that they have had seven hundred cancellations so far. There is also a bad drought, which is hurting farming, wildlife, tourism—everything. People everywhere are spending large portions of every day hunting for and hauling water.

One high government official that I have met personally,

said, "Moi has lost his confidence." Moi is at that stage. He is not only a dictator, he is an aging dictator, the worst kind.

In Lloyd Alexander's book *Westmark,* the character Florian lists all the things men will give up willingly. "Power, never."

Left to right: Randolph Whitfield, Suzanne Whitfield, Charity Mwangi, Charles Mwangi

CHAPTER THREE
1998

February 1, 1998

Six years later, Kenya is still here and has managed to survive very well without me. On previous trips, I had shipped all boxes of books and supplies by KLM cargo. They used to have missionary rates, which I was able to use, but they have discontinued them. After the boxes arrived, we (Charles, who had been assigned this chore by Charity, and I) would spend a couple of days wrestling them out of the customs warehouse while customs continued to charge us for "storage." This delightful experience, which was a real burden on Charles, usually rendered me totally mute on the way to Nyeri, hoping that Charles would forget that I, the source of trouble with customs agents, was in the car with him.

This trip, however, I was determined to bring the supplies as part of my luggage. I was extremely nervous about getting my pile of luggage past the customs officials at the airport as they are not exactly warm and fuzzy people. I picked out a woman who looked nice and got in her line. I told her the truth. I was bringing in school supplies. She looked in one suitcase and told me that they usually charged for presents, but since they were presents for children, "Just go on through."

Margaret Githinji, the Minister of Commerce and Charity's friend, and her son and daughter met me. Fortunately, they brought two cars, and the innocent son was drafted to wrestle with the luggage. We proceeded to Margaret's house for the night. In the morning, we had a leisurely breakfast. While gazing at an African garden and listening to African birds, I pondered that there is something magical about Africa that seems to loosen one's heartstrings.

Charity is sadly suffering from back problems. After spending the weekend together in Nyeri, Margaret will take Charity back to Nairobi for two weeks of hydrotherapy that we all hope will alleviate the problem.

I have always maintained that there are three things in life that are *never* convenient—birth, death, and international visitors. I feel sure Charity would agree.

Suzanne and Randy arrived for lunch. I spent the afternoon listening to very bright people discussing Kenya's problems and politics. El Niño is rarely mentioned in the United States, but here it is a deadly serious problem. The rains have flooded the northern parts of the country, ruining crops. These flooded parts of the country are subjected to cholera, malaria, and some kind of hemorrhagic fever. The roads are ruined, and getting medicine to rural areas is extremely difficult. There is massive suffering.

The consensus seems to be that most Kenyans have accepted that Moi is going to be in office for another term, and they just want to get on with their lives. There has been tribal warfare that Margaret says Moi will stop in the next few days. Parliament opens on Tuesday, so Margaret predicts that the bloodshed will be stopped by then. (Margaret's husband doesn't like her working for Moi's government, but she maintains that it is *not* Moi's country, that the country belongs to Kenyans, and that she has a perfect right to build as substantial a career as she can. While she has done so, she has suffered some interesting machinations. At the last cabinet meeting, the member sitting beside her wrote a note that said, "We are survivors, you and I.")

The plan is for Charles to drive me to school in the mornings, and a school driver will take me home in the evenings. We drove over to school this evening, and the day scholars had all gone home. The smallest boarding students had been bathed, and they were wandering around in their pajamas, robes, and slippers before being put to bed. Their faces were just as happy as I remembered.

February 6, 1998

Despite the many troubles in Kenya, for which I feel compassion, it is thankfully the case that Mount Kenya Academy is a safe and happy place. Charles drove me to school the first morning and suggested that I learn to drive myself. The thought that it was suicidal flitted briefly through my mind, but when it came down to committing suicide or irritating Charles—hey, no contest!

I drove up and down the long driveway once, clashing gears, to remind myself how to shift gears manually—and the next morning, Muthoni and I set off. (Muthoni has been working for the Mwangis for thirteen years; I first came eight years ago, and we are old friends.) Muthoni has a great sense of humor and laughs easily, but she wasn't laughing that morning. We drove the children's milk (from Charles's Jersey cows) to school and she was clutching the milk cans to keep them from spilling while peering anxiously out the window. I was too. Kenyans walk and bicycle in the road, and so do their animals. I'm afraid they were in far more danger than I was. The fact that we drove right through Kenya Police College on the way to school was nerve-wracking, but we made it. I came upon Muthoni in the office later, talking in Kikuyu and laughing. I asked her if she was telling on me, and she laughed again and said, "Yes!"

I'm now an old hand at driving and am hurtling down the road in a red Peugeot, dodging potholes with the best of them. Yesterday, there was a frightened young gray goat in the middle of the road. Every time it would head for the greenery, another vehicle would whiz by, frightening it back into the middle of the road. I pulled over and asked Muthoni to please rescue the poor goat. Muthoni looked completely baffled. About this time, the kid bolted and ran up the hill beside the road. Muthoni obviously had more experience with goats than I. Never having seen a flattened goat, I gather they are brighter than the frequently run-over possums of the American South—not that it would be hard. When we arrived back home, Muthoni charged me with driving faster than I used to.

February 8, 1998

Since I have not seen them for months, the flowers, birds, and butterflies are dazzling. The sun is shining brightly, and hopefully El Niño has loosened its grip on Kenya. The nectar-drinking sunbirds are just as iridescent as hummingbirds, and they seem to fill the same niche in nature, but they perch instead of hover. Since large numbers of flowers, bushes, and vines are massed in some manner, the perching obviously works fine.

There is a weaver bird tree (whatever kind of tree the weaver birds like) right as you enter school. Last year's dark brown nests are falling apart, or seemingly held together by cobwebs. There are a few greenish-gray, carefully woven new nests where the males who have bright yellow feathers, trimmed with black, sit close by. They are either guarding their homes and families or they are trying to attract a female with their nest-building skills. I've seen a less colorful female flitting around in a desultory fashion, so I suspect the latter.

We also had a monkey on the roof of the school causing great merriment among the children. I went out of the library to see, expecting one of the small monkeys that scamper all around like squirrels. This, however, was a big gray monkey with a white face and intelligent eyes. He seemed to be enjoying the children's laughter, looking down at them before moseying off.

Randy Whitfield's mother, Shirley, died last year, and Charity decided to commemorate her memory in the library by setting up the Shirley Whitfield Corner. Suzanne bought a rug at Nyeri market and delivered it. There is a new, bright young girl, Beatrice Wambugu, helping in the library, and we both have gotten filthy arranging shelves and books and cleaning. I wanted a large bookshelf on which to display picture books face out. A carpenter was sent to talk to me. Since I couldn't speak Kikuyu, Beatrice translated for me. I was dubious about what we would get, but in a couple of days, he delivered a great, long, low, painted bookshelf that was absolutely perfect both for displaying books face out and for enabling little children to easily reach them.

Randy Whitfield Sr., who is eighty-nine, has remarried. His bride Julia is eighty. They are very happy, and they are coming to visit the family, and the school to see the memorial—which is now completed and looks quite nice. Creating the Shirley Whitfield Corner was a pleasure and an honor, as she was one of Aunt Adah's dearest friends, and I have known her since childhood. Randy Sr. donated money to buy new books, and they look lovely on display on the new bookshelf. It is a fitting tribute to a wonderful woman.

I am very nervous about the large furry African spiders that have many places to hide in the library. I was teaching a group of Standard Ones who suddenly started wiggling their fingers at me. I wondered what was going on but the wiggling fingers began to point at my jacket. I looked down and a large spider was sitting on my lapel like a broach. To their delight, I screamed and hastily disrobed.

February 12, 1998

Jesse Jackson has been to Kenya as President Clinton's envoy. He visited the hospitals in Rift Valley, where there has been tribal fighting. He expressed outrage over the victims, and he called on President Moi to tour Rift Valley to stop the fighting. He was also closeted with Moi for several hours. A few days later, Moi and his entourage toured the Rift Valley where Moi announced that his visit had *not* been prompted by Jackson's visit, because "it had already been scheduled."

Everyone is horrified over the fighting, and the clergy are speaking out and leading demonstrations. The clergy in Kenya are bold and seemingly united on the side of the angels—a force to be reckoned with. When the students at Kenyatta University peacefully demonstrated, the government shut it down—*again.* (I don't think I have ever been here when the university didn't get shut down on some pretext or another.)

I am now teaching classes. Last week I was helping set up the Shirley Whitfield Corner of the library in memory of Randy's mother. Randy is a Westminster graduate. He is an ophthalmologist who came to Kenya with his wife Suzanne in the early seventies and stayed. He trained paramedics to perform cataract surgery—much needed by the elderly in this country of sunshine. For this work, he received a MacArthur Genius Grant.

Charles had bought the Nyeri Kindergarten to launch Charity on her career in 1978. Charity hired Suzanne

Whitfield in 1980 to teach at the Kindergarten while another teacher, Janet Dillard, returned to the United States with her missionary husband for their furlough. Meanwhile, the parents were urging Charity to continue the Kindergarten into Standard One as Charity was already shining as an educator. A classroom was built on the Nyeri Kindergarten campus. Charity decided to continue to build up a school.

Charles bought a farm outside of Nyeri and helped Charity turn it into Mount Kenya Academy, building classrooms, dormitories, and altering the farmhouse and other buildings for the school, which opened in 1982. Charity added one Standard a year until, in eight years, she had a complete primary school that shone from the beginning. Suzanne worked with her in establishing this school—and so did Janet Dillard upon her return to Kenya from her family's missionary furlough. That was a wonderful educational triumvirate. Randy is the one who suggested establishing a connection with Westminster, which Suzanne, who had also attended Westminster, pursued. She persuaded Linda Grady to come over a summer as a visiting teacher, and the rest is history.

After returning to teaching here from a long hiatus, I find the children are delightful. One child smiles at every word I say, and one tiny girl is concentrating so hard that she frowns the entire time. Life for her is earnest. The always welcoming faculty, however, can find things about my return to be amusing. When I went to the computer room to send an email, the person who had sent an email before me had entitled it, "Crazy Americans!" As I am the only American presently on the faculty, I could only ponder the inspiration for such.

Suzanne came to pick me up at Charity's yesterday. We visited schools where we have started libraries. First we stopped by a farm and picked up Sara Sessions, the farm's owner. Then we stopped by a school close to her farm called Karacheni. We passed a group of smiling waving little children, and when we stopped to take their picture, they fled in terror. At Karacheni, they had a couple hundred books locked in a cabinet. That doesn't seem like much, but that is exactly how we started at other schools with actual libraries—rooms with tables, chairs, shelves, and *books*.

From there, we drove to an area so remote that the farmers have trouble with wild animals—including elephants. We visited Nyange Primary School, which used to be so poor that teachers hated to be posted there. That was before Sara Sessions got involved. She succeeded in getting the British High Commission to build a classroom building—complete with concrete floor and glass in the windows. She enlisted another organization, and the school now has two good classroom buildings. She also helped the school plant a field of high quality grass, and now they can bale and sell the hay. A bag of books had arrived at Nyange, so their library has begun. Sara wants to help them with another building—a room which will serve as a library. I am so impressed with her work. We returned to Sara's house for tea, and afterwards Suzanne and I proceeded on alone.

After tea, we visited Lusoi Primary School. The Children's School in Atlanta and my sister-in-law Peg Richards, who teaches there, have sent enough books to Lusoi to furnish their library. They now have a room set aside for a library *and* a librarian, Mercy Munyi.

Mercy has been there ever since I first visited Lusoi in 1992. She is absolutely *wonderful,* and I want to clone her for other schools. Lusoi has been planting and selling hay for a number of years. They use the money to buy books. By Kenyan standards, thanks to The Children's School, their library is quite extensive. Mercy said that she had been "very low" last year because of the total lack of discipline under the old headmaster. This year, however, they have a young, enthusiastic headmaster who had attended Lusoi himself. He has brought things under control since the new school year started in January. Mercy has worked very hard with little encouragement. I am just amazed at her commitment. The library room is rather pitiful with dust filtering in from every crack. Mercy has cloth squares with which she covers all the books at the end of every school day. And the books are checked out. We visited Standard Eight, and the students were completely perplexed by my accent. However, when I asked to see what they were reading, they all dove into their bags and sacks and pulled out their books. I went around the room looking at the books they were reading—quite an array. I stopped and chatted with the barefoot boy who was reading Lloyd Alexander's *Time Cat.* (I pondered how that book would give him glimpses of other civilizations. Books are wonderful at enlarging children's worlds and stimulating imagination.)

Next, we went to Iragathagi Primary School. One thing I have seen very little of in Kenya is children with disabilities. I thought it was probably because it is so hard for them to survive. However, Iragathagi is right next to a crippled children's hospital, and the children from the hospital attend school there. Suzanne brought their Standard Eight into the room serving as a library, and there were two girls with severe disabilities in the class. (One appeared to be a thalidomide child with stumps for hands and feet.) Both girls were quite bright, and the child with stumps for limbs was reading difficult books. I showed her quite a number of books that I thought she would enjoy reading. I left pondering that only through imagination and stories is she able to enter into experiences that are impossible for her physically. There are many wonderful people at this school working to improve the lot of these children. It was an honor to meet them.

These primary schools only go through Standard Eight. Young people without the resources to attend high school finish their education upon completion of primary school. One of Suzanne's experiences reveals the enthusiasm for reading the library books that Children's Literature for Children has contributed to the schools close to Suzanne's home. She is a runner and runs through the Kenyan countryside. She is frequently stopped by the local primary school graduates asking her for books to read. She has begun to carry a few books with her to share with young people that she meets while running.

February 21, 1998

Charity, Suzanne, and I came to Mombasa for midterm break. All along the horizon, the waves are breaking against the coral reef that protects Mombasa beaches. Suzanne says the reef keeps the sharks away, although they occasionally get into Mombasa harbor and eat a few people—but not here. That's comforting.

I am trying to collect enough cowry shells (which once were used for money) to take to my Campbell students when I return to Atlanta. I never seem to learn that nature is rarely the same from day to day. Yesterday morning, the beach was covered with cowry shells. I collected until I got tired, telling myself that I could collect more this morning. When I came out at the exact same time, there was nary a cowry shell to be seen. Yesterday morning there were monkeys all over the place. Today, none. What I did see was a large blue heron stalking about in the grass eating insects. The Mombasa insects are so large that the heron could enjoy a nutritious diet without ever getting his feet wet. I am afraid of the large spiders and centipedes, but I met a *humongous* snail with a gorgeous shell.

Charity's daughter Betty joined us last night for the weekend. We fly back on Sunday so I can meet my 8:00 class on Monday.

The monkeys came back. A mother monkey was sitting on a branch over the path with a *tiny* baby. She let me approach quite close while I congratulated her. I got the impression that this was her first baby because she all but let me hold it. She seemed to think it was entirely proper that I was as impressed as she seemed to be. She was a gray, black-faced monkey, but the baby's face and ears were pink. It looked like a tiny, wizened white person. It was interested in its surroundings and was scrambling to get out on the branch, but it was very uncoordinated. Mama pulled it back and held it, and I glimpsed the remains of the umbilical cord. It finally settled down and began to suck on its tiny paws. The mother may learn to be more leery of people, but I quite enjoyed our visit.

Last weekend I was privileged to learn a little more about wedding celebrations in Kenya. Charity took me to a Kikuyu wedding. The daughter of friends was marrying a young man from the United States. His family and best man were all from Washington, D.C. This family was introduced to the large gathering, they were seated in a tent, and then we all had a feast. The bride was nowhere in sight because she was hiding. Tradition calls for the groom and his friends to search for her later. First, the groom's mother had to present the bride's family with traditional presents. Because she had no women with her, a call went out for women "to be the Americans." No one wanted to be the Americans. Everyone scattered, so people got drafted—me included. (I couldn't very well say I didn't want to be an American.) I really couldn't follow what was happening, but I got swept up in events. We lined up out of sight with all the gifts. The groom and best man led the parade with a sheep and a goat—poor things (the animals, I mean). These young men were not expert animal handlers, and they ended up dragging them along on three legs. I became quite grateful that my "gift" was inanimate. A former teacher from Charity's childhood, Ann Ndegwa, was in front of me carrying a big gourd of beer, held by a leather strap across her forehead. The line of people, with Kikuyu dancers bringing up the rear, stopped while someone made a windy speech. I noticed this lovely woman's neck trembling beneath her heavy load. I came up behind her and propped up the gourd. The speech went on for so long that I finally muttered, "Hurry *up*." Then I got worried that I had been incredibly rude. At last, we were allowed to "arrive," and were greeted by the bride's family. I was embraced, kissed on both cheeks, and told that now I was a "real Kikuyu." (I thought I already was.) The young men were no better at finding the bride than they were at wrangling animals.

March 4, 1998

The political situation in Kenya is deteriorating. The clergy here are very active and brave. The moderator of the East African Presbyterian Church, the Anglican bishop, and the Catholic bishop are collectively preaching against the detention and torture of people who speak out against the present government of Daniel arap Moi. Christianity is strong in Kenya. The churches are packed on Sundays and a multitude of people are out dressed in their Sunday best.

At school, I was working alone in the library when a few girls sidled up to me, and the ringleader asked me if I knew the name of the woman who kept returning to the south to help other slaves run away. I told them that she was probably thinking of Harriet Tubman. I turned in my chair and was able to pick *Harriet Tubman: Guide to Freedom* off the shelf behind me. The girl said, "That's who it is. I just couldn't remember her name...(pause)...I admire her courage." She took the book, and then she asked me if my parents would care if I worked with black people.

With absolutely no warning, I was able to pay tribute to my parents. I said, "My parents taught me to love all people, and because of them, I am able to have lovely friends—*like you.*" I was rewarded with warm smiles.

Mount Kenya Academy—under Charity's leadership— is a stellar institution. This school has a happy aura. The elements, including discipline and high expectations, have found a wonderful balance here. The children have lovely manners. When they want to talk to me, they usually preface it with "Excuse me..." I may have five children addressing me at the same time, but they are all chiming, "Excuse me..." The children in their uniforms (another factor in discipline, I believe) are just so bright-eyed and charming. Whenever we are looking at each other—frequently—I am reminded of the French poet Paul Éluard's observation that when all eyes are facing each other, they are sharing the wonder of being outside of time.

Leading the parade to the opening of Grace Chapel, Cindy Candler with the pulpit Bible, followed by Charity Mwangi, Headmistress, and William Muhungu, Chairman of the Board of Directors

CHAPTER FOUR
1999

February 2, 1999

Yesterday, after recovering for a couple of days from jet lag, Rebecca Rogers, a young woman from Chicago who accompanied me, and I were joined by Rebecca Njogu and Tabitha Mwangi, teachers from Mount Kenya Academy. We all paid a visit to Milimani Primary School, a school just up the road from Charity's house. Children's Literature for Children has started a collection of books at the school and plans to continue building up their small library. The floors of Milimani are dirt; the walls are wood. There is no electricity or running water. The windows have no glass, but the wooden shutters are closed to keep out the cool wind and dust, as this is the dry and dusty season. As a result, the children are working in semidarkness. We all bumped up in the Mount Kenya Academy van. Rebecca Rogers had the foresight to suggest that we bring candy from the U.S. for the children. We piled out of the van bearing candy, laminated bookmarks (cut out by the hundreds by Betty Dodds), and stickers.

Since they speak Kikuyu and don't study English until Standard Four, the children couldn't understand a word we said, but we became instant successes by passing out bookmarks and "sweets." The little ones received fairly large suckers. A classroom teacher, who serves as the designated librarian, was given the stickers with the suggestion that she place a sticker on the individual's bookmark whenever the child finished a book. Rebecca Rodgers suggested that we give children one sticker on their bookmarks to get them started. Stickers have universal appeal to the young, and the children all seemed to enjoy this business immensely. By the time we left, the students had been dismissed to walk home to eat lunch. Our three hundred new best friends waved with great enthusiasm. (I wish we could do more.)

After Milimani, we went to Naro Moru to eat lunch with Randy and Suzanne Whitfield, who have moved up the road to a newer location but an older house. They have a charming red brick house with a cedar shingle roof. The grounds are beautiful, and we took a long walk around the property accompanied by a pack of enthusiastic adult dogs and one even more enthusiastic puppy called Buddha. Part of the walk skirted the beautiful Nairobi River, which is really a stream this close to the headwaters. The Whitfields have harnessed water power to pump water up to the house. Suzanne has a large vegetable garden. The whole place is delightful, but Charity says I wouldn't believe how rundown the place was before Suzanne went to work on it. The children, Eston and Louisa, who are attending Antioch College in Ohio, have their own separate cottage.

At school, the big news is the new chapel. A chapel has been given by Cindy Candler of First Presbyterian Church of Atlanta, and indeed, it is almost finished. It is the source of great excitement. The inside walls of stone have been completed, and the tiles for the floor are piled by the entrance. Charles is supervising the construction. He showed me the door frames being unloaded. He went to Karatina this afternoon to check on the church pews. Charity went to Nairobi this morning to meet with the people in the head office of the Presbyterian Church East Africa to discuss the dedication that will occur on March 11. A contingent of members from First Presbyterian Church of Atlanta—Cindy's church—will also attend this auspicious occasion.

February 6, 1999

I am awash in lilac-breasted rollers. Of all the beautiful birds in the world, it is among the fairest. Rebecca and I are visiting Masai Mara, and we have seen a number of the rollers. We flew in yesterday at noon. I haven't been here since visiting with Johnny in 1992. This time we are staying at the Serena Lodge situated on a high bluff overlooking the plain, which is literally teeming with animals. The grounds of the Lodge itself are protected by an electric fence. Inside the fence, these grounds are highly populated with gray rock hyraxes, a small mammal. The first one I came across was quite tame and perfectly willing to be photographed. Little did I know that they are inclined to sun themselves on the lounge chairs by the pool and disinclined to move for the hotel guests. They must be fairly intelligent to have moved into the local resort and taken it over, rather than dwelling on the plain as hors d'oeuvres for large predators.

We had a run-in with another resort dweller. Yesterday, we sat down for lunch in the delightful, airy dining room—too airy as it turned out. I was looking down at my plate, when Rebecca screamed and leaped across the room. I sat there baffled until I turned my head to the left. A large gray baboon was sitting within inches of me on his haunches. He appeared to grin at me, and he reached out a large gray hand and helped himself to my roll. He caused a sensation in the dining room among the guests. I quickly joined Rebecca on the other side of the room. As neither of us was inclined to *ever* sit with our backs to the window again, we ate our remaining meals side by side with our backs to the walls for the duration of our trip.

It's hard to believe the African plains are real. One would travel this far just to see giraffes in their own territory, but the abundance of wildlife is mind-boggling.

I never realized how much a large portion of the animals resemble rocks. There are large, black rocks in and around the river, and the hippos blend right in—though why they need camouflage is a mystery. The game driver told us that they just chomp down on crocodiles that bother them. Warthogs look like rocks; hyenas look like rocks—especially if they are lolling in a muddy hole—and elephants resemble large, stately rocks. There is plenty of color elsewhere, however. My favorite sighting was of two tawny lionesses who had a large disorderly collection of cubs following them. They apparently had the cubs at the same time. The cubs were very vocal, and the mothers were answering with deep growls. One cub at the rear got tired of the journey and sat down. One lioness continued with the cubs, and the other lioness sat down and waited patiently. As we were driving away, the cub ran up beside her. Life and death are strikingly mingled. One Thomson's gazelle had chosen a grassy spot littered with bones to lie in.

We were also driven to another part of the Mara River where the migrating animals have beaten down paths in order to cross the river. There are enormous crocodiles lurking there. The pictures of such creatures do not have the impact of the living reptile. One crocodile was lying with its mouth agape. "To cool off," I was told. I puzzled over this as the cool water was lapping its toes, but I suppose the crocodile knows best what it is doing since its race is far more ancient than my own.

February 13, 1999

Rebecca has returned home, and I am teaching for another month until the chapel gets dedicated. The Kenyan universities have been shut down again. This time it is over the Karura Forest outside of Nairobi. Some of this public land has been confiscated and is being developed, and the developers are being secretly sheltered by the government. The students organized and decided to show up at the forest with tree seedlings to plant to protest the confiscation of public lands. Guards met the students at the gate leading into the forest and beat them savagely.

Professor Wangari Maathai, a woman respected around the world as a leader of the Green Belt Movement, went with the students the next time, and the guards beat her.

By now, all the students at all the universities have begun supporting the cause, and they are going in large groups to the forest. More savage beatings. The picture of a college girl lying unconscious in a pool of her own blood, beaten by police in riot gear, is unforgettable. Everyone is thoroughly outraged, and now the churches are getting involved. The clergy are going to march to Karura Forest.

"And a little child shall lead them." The youth have led the way.

At least, they led until Moi closed the universities. Moi also said he didn't know what all the fuss was about because other developments had been built in former forests. One of the "protectors" of the developers further enraged the clergy by saying, "Even Jesus wouldn't be able to enter the forest."

February 25, 1999

I've just returned from checking on the construction of Grace Chapel. At the moment almost nothing is happening. I'd like to think that it is because it is close to lunch hour, but it is probably because Charles is not there. The three stained glass windows to be installed are of a child leading the lion and the lamb, given by Cindy Candler, which is to go in the center of the front wall; the other two, which are to be installed in the corners of the back wall, are Jesus blessing the children, given by Cindy in honor of Westminster, and the "Good Shepherd" given by me in honor of Charity. These windows are presently stuck in Nairobi. The agent keeps calling and giving reports on the windows—but he hasn't shaken them loose yet. I suspect it will require a number of bribes before they are released. The stress level, particularly for Charles, is heating up. Because Cindy Candler, the donor, has invited a group from First Presbyterian Church—led by the pastor George Wirth—for the dedication, there is an approaching deadline.

The gift of this chapel is part of the 150th anniversary celebration of First Presbyterian Church of Atlanta. During one of the early planning meetings for this celebration, George Wirth said pensively, "I wish we could build a church somewhere." This struck a chord with Cindy, who was on the committee and had visited Mount Kenya Academy, and she decided to give the chapel to the school as part of the celebration. It took over three years to bring the plan to fruition, and the dedication is to be the final piece of the 150th celebration.

February 26, 1999

Next week, Charity and I will go to Nairobi—not my favorite place. Despite the deadly traffic, Charles makes me unfasten my seat belt upon entering Nairobi so that the car-jackers won't shoot me while I am fumbling to unfasten my seat belt. As the theory goes, I can leap out of the car quickly if my seat belt is unlatched, saying, "Here, take my place." Fortunately, we haven't had to put this plan into practice.

On Thursday morning, we pick up Cindy and Martha Griffin, the former Westminster teacher who brought Cindy to visit Mount Kenya Academy in the first place. We will cool our heels in Nairobi on Thursday night, since there is no room for them at the Outspan in Nyeri, and drive to Nyeri on Friday morning. They will be spending a few days before the rest of the official delegation arrives. The others arrive next Wednesday, and the dedication will take place on Thursday.

March 11, 1999

The chapel has been dedicated. It was a beautiful day and occasion. Charles bullied the construction crew into finishing the chapel in the nick of time; school staff was still scrubbing the tile floor the night before.

The celebrants included many dignitaries of the East African Presbyterian Church led by Jessie Kamau, an older pastor and leader of the church, along with First Presbyterian's pastor, George Wirth. They gathered and prayed in the staff room before the event. Everyone formed into a column to parade out of the entrance of the school, up the road, into the entrance of the chapel. This parade was led by a glowing Cindy, who was carrying the pulpit Bible. She was followed by Charity Mwangi, the headmistress, and William Muhungu, the Chairman of the Board of Mount Kenya Academy; the pastors; Charles and their daughter Betty; the First Presbyterian visitors, whom I joined; the other visiting dignitaries; students, parents, and faculty. I may have mixed up the order, but it was a substantial parade. It stopped for the official knocking on the double doors and blessing before filling the chapel up to the brim. The ceremony itself featured a sermon by George Wirth and talks, speeches, and lovely singing by the girls' choir, under the leadership and piano playing of the school's music teacher, Janet Dillard.

At the conclusion, everyone walked out of the church and gathered around while Cindy uncovered the plaque commemorating both the date and her gift:

THIS CHAPEL IS GIVEN
TO THE GLORY OF GOD
BY
CINDY CANDLER
FIRST PRESBYTERIAN
CHURCH OF ATLANTA
GEORGIA
MARCH 11, 1999

Christopher Paul Curtis with students of Burgeret Primary School

CHAPTER FIVE
2001

May 17, 2001

Rwanda was not where I intended to go. I flew Sabena
through Brussels because the fare was the cheapest. I don't
recommend it. I was not impressed by either the plane or
the Brussels airport, but I was astonished to discover while
boarding the plane that we had a layover in Rwanda, the last
place in the world that I wanted to enter. I'd have preferred
North Korea.

As we flew in, Rwanda was breathtakingly beautiful. Yet
what literally took my breath away was that I was looking
at the actual physical place where, within recent memory,
the massive atrocities occurred. I remember someone saying
that there were no demons left in hell—that they were all in
Rwanda. (And 125,000 of them are in Rwandan prisons.)

Strangely, before Rwanda exploded, a woman came to
visit me at my home in Atlanta. I welcomed her because she
had some connection to the Whitfields. I shortly began to
regret the welcome as she had recently returned from a trip
to see the gorillas in Rwanda, and she bent my ear about the
strange feelings she had in Rwanda. She said that she felt a

pervasive sense of evil, and that she couldn't wait to get out of the country. I thought she was nuts. She was prescient.

My seatmate on the plane was from Kigali. He was a charming young man who showed me his passport. It looked exactly like my passport except for the color. Only a different color separated us. He is a scientist who was in Europe during the massacres. His family in Rwanda had survived. I couldn't bear to ask him if he was a Hutu. Somehow to ask would be to enter the mindset from which the evil sprang.

After several hours of eternity in Rwanda, we reboarded the plane, and a group of young men settled in the seats around me. They told me that they were prosecutors from the United States Attorney General's Office. The U.S. government was not paying them but did give them unpaid leave to help the Attorney General of Rwanda. They were there, not to prosecute war criminals, but to help the Rwandan government begin to get a handle on the task of processing 125,000 prisoners. The country is so devastated that I cannot begin to fathom the problems. I was told that the young man across from me was a computer whiz who had set up a program to help with processing.

What a relief to finally land in Kenya. How I love my friends and their beautiful country! The last time I was here, Kenya was in the middle year of a three-year drought. Everything was bone dry and covered with dust. Now, after ample rain, it is verdant. The crops look healthy and the rivers are splashing. There even seem to be more birds. The birds of East Africa are delightful. I am particularly fond of the bright yellow weaver birds. Their nests are like woven hanging gourds.

Charity, as I've explained, is the headmistress of Mount Kenya Academy. Sometimes I work in her office just for the quiet. The other day it was anything but. The weaver bird—inches away—kept hammering on the window. No doubt he saw his reflection. He was so noisy and determined to rid the neighborhood of this interloper that I returned to the peace and quiet of the child-filled library.

Walking down the steps of the school entrance and hearing the children singing as I walked into the assembly, I felt as if I had never left. There is something very special about communal singing by children. It is an entirely positive experience. The songs, a combination of children's hymns and cheerful camp tunes, bind the singers together. The sound of children singing is lovely. (Many children in the United States almost never experience communal singing any more, except perhaps at camp, if they are lucky.)

The bright faces were also the same—except for the extremely curious looks from Standards One and Two, but I had even read to them in Nyeri Kindergarten. (The combined nursery school and kindergarten is on a separate campus in town. It is directed by Wanjiru Sababady, Charity's sister.) I had read *McDuff Moves In* by Rosemary Wells. If the tiny children couldn't understand me, they could understand the large, clear, and emotionally expressive pictures by Susan Jeffers. All children can understand the little lost dog and his longing for a home.

There is no need for air conditioning or heating in the Central Highlands of Kenya. The combination of being on the equator and seven thousand feet up produces the freshest, crispest air I have ever known. Opening the windows in the morning is a sensory delight. Night falls very quickly and a sweater and a fire (which I haven't laid) feel cozy. Nights are quiet with time to read, write letters, and enjoy conversation with friends. Those of you young enough to want crowds, bright lights, and loud music would find this atmosphere a tad staid, but it is heavenly.

The way of life in the United States has become not just hurried, but frenetic. Perhaps all the frantic activity makes us feel indispensable? Perhaps it covers up an emptiness? A delegation from the Presbyterian Church of East Africa arrived to deliver the new school chaplain, accompanied by luggage and assorted friends and relatives. There was considerable standing around while moving from place to place, and somehow I found myself at the front of the group "getting on with it." The more leisurely "it" was happening behind me. There are other ways of doing things, and I quite enjoy them when I can turn off the internal buzz saw.

May 19, 2001

This morning Charity and I went to the church service in the lovely new Grace Chapel.

During the service, the children come up to the front by age groups. The youngest sing songs and sit down. As we progress up the age groups, the songs and rhythms grow more complex. The Africans I've met seem so gifted musically, and I have pondered where the wonderful sense of rhythm originates. Is the mother's heartbeat stronger and therefore more strongly imprinted on the baby in the womb? There's no way of knowing, and I'm on shaky ground here, so I'll leave it alone. Let it suffice to say that I can't even hold a beat while clapping. Charity was obviously trying not to laugh at me during the service, but I could tell she was amused. Fortunately, we were sitting in the back row so I couldn't disgrace myself in front of all the students, but the ones who looked back were tickled. The children and the songs were spirited and meaningful. Praising God in such a lovely environment simply has to sink into souls. It sank into mine.

I still love observing the birds. The wagtails, who do just that, rock across the grass. Two large birds with loud, raucous cries hang out at the Mwangis' house. I was trying to see where the racket was originating when Charles told me to look at the top of the house. There they were at the pinnacle: two gray birds with downward-curving beaks who obviously belong to the stork family. Charles lent me his copy of *A Field Guide to the Birds of East Africa,* but I haven't looked them up yet. The sunbirds also have downward-curving beaks. They use them to sip nectar from the flowers. They seem to fill the same niche in nature that hummingbirds fill at home, but the sunbirds perch instead of hover. There is a beautiful, long, trumpet-shaped, hanging red flower whose petals curve up around the edges but whose yellow heart is underneath. I watched a small, light brown sunbird with a blue tail hanging upside down sipping nectar. It was the female. Two of them were flitting around fearlessly close to me. The other was obviously the male, because he had a brighter blue tail and iridescent turquoise feathers neatly shining along the tops of his wings.

And the doves! I don't see them all the time, but I hear them all the time. They have a distinctive call that represents Kenya to me. I love that sound with a passion. Whenever I hear it in a movie, for example, I always get homesick for Kenya—but now is now, and it is a lovely part of my life.

The sunbirds are obviously not averse to getting a little protein. One of them flew down to the ground with a large, caterpillar-looking insect. It settled on a brick on the patio and proceeded to peck this bug to death with its now inconveniently downward-curved beak. It had such difficulty that I laughed aloud. Nevertheless, it persisted and successfully ate this treasure.

May 20, 2001

The Whitfields' newest house is one of the most pleasant, beautiful spots on the planet. The house has some sort of huge, fold-back French doors that stay open from dawn to dusk. With terraces and decks all around, the house has as much outside as inside. The dogs, who are all happy, of course, wander about; the birds fly in and out. Suzanne has a flock of geese, all white with one gray, who are strolling about on the green grass nibbling a little salad. They set up an unholy racket if strangers approach—they serve as great "watch geese" guarding the premises.

I remember when we tromped down from an old, empty farmhouse on the ridge, crossed the river, and wandered around in the thorny bushes while Suzanne told us where the new house would be and how the windows would face Mount Kenya—which they now do. Suzanne can view Mount Kenya from her bathtub. The house is built of stone; flowering vines have covered all the arbors in purple, orange, and white. The gardens are lovely. For safety from fire, the kitchen is a detached building. This house seems as if it has always been here.

That old farmhouse on the ridge has now been renovated and turned into the home of Kenyan flower growers, Tim and Maggie. Tim grows flowers for Europe—lilies and roses—so Suzanne's house is also overflowing with flowers. Suzanne calls them "rejects," but no one could ever discern it. Suzanne's friend and Randy's sister, Croom, is presently visiting them in their wonderful house.

Suzanne has decided that we will all go on an adventure in honor of Croom's visit. Suzanne invited Charity and me to fly with them to our present location, a tented camp in Meru National Park. We are in Joy Adamson's stomping ground. She wrote *Born Free* and *Living Free* about the lion cub, Elsa, that she raised and released back into the wild here. I am sitting in an airy honeymoon suite by myself overlooking

Meru Plain right where Elsa used to hang out on the rocks. One rock formation is known as "Elsa's Kopje." I've just watched a couple of giraffes amble by.

Meru Park is "Dove Heaven." The whole plain rings with their calls from one end to the other. Coming from distances, you can't distinguish individual calls. It's like the sound of the plain itself—an indescribable but gentle background noise. It began when the sun rose. Meru National Park is dry, with rivers that arise from the glaciers on Mount Kenya running through it. It's green now because they've had rains recently, but the area has a harsh history. We went on a game drive and were shown a place where ivory tusks used to be hidden in caves. I was told by Daniel, our game driver, that Somalis have invaded from the east and gone on an orgy of killing. The wildlife has been decimated. This camp is only a couple of years old and is relatively small. Daniel also said the park is now well guarded. We saw a large military type plane flying around, and he said it was the National Wildlife Service.

There's game here, enough to find animals on a game drive—but certainly not an abundance. My favorite sighting was a beautiful, healthy lioness draped elegantly at the top of a smaller kopje. Her three cubs were with her. They momentarily tried to drape, but they were far too playful to stay still. An endearing cub peered at us from the far side—the safe side—of his mother. His ears, still too large for his face, stood out against the sky. Surely, these are Elsa's relatives. (I suppose, with a dearth of grazing animals, all these grasses shelter and feed birds.) Mughwango Plain will always be "Dove Plain" to me. Our game drive was basically a bird drive—a wonderful array.

My aerie, where I'm enjoying early morning tea, faces east. This is Meru. There is nothing but plain between Kenya and Somalia. This area has been overrun with bandits bringing in guns—many of which have ended up in the hands of criminals in Nairobi. The government is struggling to get a handle on it.

Suzanne, Charity, and I climbed Mughwango Hill late yesterday afternoon. It is the site of George Adamson's first camp. We also saw his favorite fishing spot yesterday. A knowledgeable guide, George led us up. It was fun, but I stopped short of the pinnacle, which was a sheer rock climb to the tip top. My intrepid friends climbed the last bit, of course. As we slipped and slid our way down the "hill," George virtually went down backwards to help a gray-haired old lady who shall remain nameless. For those of you who have ever had the experience, it was like climbing a small Stone Mountain—with baboons.

May 30, 2001

Cindy Candler and Nancy Rigby arrived on Thursday for a week-long visit. Nancy arrived in town, and the next day she whisked us off to the office of the head of the East and South Africa division of Coca-Cola. Two movers and shakers had definitely arrived in Nairobi. We spent Thursday night at the Muthaiga Club, and Friday morning we sallied forth at the beginning of a long—*very* long—day. Early in the morning, we headed for the headquarters of the Presbyterian Church of East Africa to meet with Reverend Rukenya, the Secretary-General. After visiting with him, we traveled in the Mount Kenya Academy van to Kikuyu to meet with Plauson Kuria, the president of Presbyterian University. Many of my friends can affirm that I do not respond swiftly in emergencies. As Nancy, Cindy, Charity, and I were being chauffeured by the friendly school driver in the van from Nairobi to Kikuyu, I was looking at a group of large, pink chemical tanks off to our right. Suddenly there was a loud explosion. Nancy instantly perceived that the van had exploded, and she leaped out and was standing safely by the side of the road while I sat there staring at the pink tanks wondering if we were going to be engulfed in a chemical detonation. Fortunately, it was a vehicular steam explosion, not a gas one, and Charity and I joined Nancy and Cindy by the side of the road.

Charity organized another ride for us to meet with Plauson Kuria, so Nancy, Cindy, and I continued on with a drafted local driver, leaving Charity and our first driver to deal with the broken-down van. By the time we had admired everything at Presbyterian University—including a houseful of adolescent chickens—Charity pulled up in the van, having managed to get the thankfully small problem fixed. We went back to Nairobi to eat a late lunch at the Norfolk Hotel before heading off to an afternoon meeting with William Egbe at his Coca-Cola office. Nancy impressively directed the meeting. Then we got caught in the Nairobi evening rush hour, which has to be experienced to be believed. As Charity's daughter Betty warns, "You *must* be in either Nyeri or Nairobi by 9:00 PM—*not* somewhere in between." We, however, were not.

After picking up Jennifer Ngugi, the computer teacher, who had collected some computer equipment in town, we left Nairobi late and were tootling down the highway. BAM! Another explosion occurred. Unlike yours truly, Nancy is great in an emergency. She had the usually stuck van door open in an instant for us all to leap out onto a very narrow shoulder of the road with extremely dangerous traffic. We were all pouring our expensive bottled water from the Muthaiga Club into the radiator, hoping the van could limp to Thika when a handsome young Baptist missionary—a blessing on his head—stopped. He gave Nancy, Cindy, and me a lift to the Blue Post Hotel on the highway outside of Thika. We promptly retired to the bar.

The expensive water allowed the van to chug up to the parking lot of the hotel, but Charity refused to ride in it another inch. She called the Muthaiga Club and asked for them to send us a taxi. She went to Thika to get the van repaired while we continued waiting in the bar.

Finally, after several hours, the taxi arrived—an ex-London, black, boxy taxi. The now-returned Charity, and the rest of us, and all our luggage piled into the back with the taxi driver and the school van driver in the front. After some discussion over the fact that it was an hour back to the Muthaiga Club and an hour and a half to Nyeri, we decided to press on.

First, however, the taxi driver informed us that he didn't have any gas. We had to drive into Thika, several kilometers behind the Blue Post Hotel, to get gas. It was now late and crowded. Because it was so dark, the crowds seemed ominous. The gas stations were all packed. By the time we succeeded in getting gas, we all had to stop off at the Blue Post Hotel again. It was well past the time Betty said we must be *off* the road before we got *on* the road.

The taxi driver was terrible. He had very dim headlights; he was extremely nervous about venturing through dark, bandit-infested country to Nyeri; he was clashing gears and swerving all over the road. Plus he had a series of emotions wafting from the back seat—changing from laughter to prayers and back again. Charity reported later that she was praying, "Please God, we've had enough..." when— CLUNK, CLUNK, CLUNK.

At first, we five women stayed in the car while the driver tried to change the flat tire; but, of course, that proved to be impossible with all our weight, so we piled out. The taxi driver, who was a nervous wreck by this point, sure that we were going to be attacked by bandits, couldn't get the spare tire onto the car. And, as Nancy dryly observed, instead of putting the lugs into his pockets as our husbands would have done, he dropped them in the gravel. Our van driver finally took the tire away from the shaking taxi driver and put it on the car while Cindy held the one dim flashlight. Then "the great lug search" began by this pitiful flashlight.

Finally, we all climbed back in. Charity was extremely

distressed by this point, but we clashed gears on up the road. At last, sometime after midnight, we arrived in Nyeri at the Outspan where Nancy and Cindy were staying. Charles was standing in the middle of the driveway. The taxi promptly had another puncture in the driveway, but we escaped once again into the bar where Cindy massively understated, "I need a Tusker."

As for Jennifer, she slept through the whole thing.

May 31, 2001

There are some beautiful watercolors of Mount Kenya at the Outspan Hotel that Cindy had seen on a 1999 visit. When she came back, she was determined to buy one. She found out the name of the artist, Timothy Brooks. Suzanne learned that he lives outside of Nanyuki, so Cindy, Nancy, Charity, and I went on a quest to find this artist. On the way, we saw a camel caravan with one camel driver by the side of the road. We stopped to take a picture, when the camel driver ran very fast toward the car with a long club and a vicious look on his face—prompting a hasty retreat.

Timothy Brooks lives in a quite odd sort of stick-and-board house that he has built himself. I loved the outdoor bathtub where he can bathe and look at the stars.

During this visit, he took us into his studio and started showing us some watercolors he had painted of Mount Kenya. They were lovely, and Cindy bought two. I started thinking what a perfect wedding present it would make for Mary Evelyn and Scott, so I bought two also, one as a wedding gift, and one for John and me.

June 5, 2001

Nancy Rigby and Cindy Candler left on Saturday night. Charity and I spent the night at the Muthaiga Club. Charity's father, who is a hundred years old, is not doing well, so Charity went back to Nyeri on Sunday morning with her sister, Lydiah. I stayed in town. Michael, the driver, picked me up to go to the airport that afternoon to meet Ashley Bryan. As we were approaching the booth to pay the airport tax, I realized that all I had was a thousand Rwanda shillings and a couple of U.S. dollars. Michael fortunately had some money.

I met Ashley, and we had an uneventful trip to Nyeri, thank goodness. Ashley—who, in addition to his children's books, puppets, and stained glass windows made of sea glass does gorgeous oil paintings of flowers—arrived at the Mwangis' house before dark. I was eager for him to see Charity's beautiful, profuse flower garden before the sun went down (blam—at seven o'clock, year round). He was properly enchanted. Monday morning we went to school, and he was immediately put to work.

Ashley recited poetry in his inimitable fashion for assembly at school. He then began talking with students as the classes met in the library. Each Standard is divided in half so that teachers meet with about fifteen students at a time—an ideal class size that fits around two long tables in the library. The students were rather shy about talking with Ashley during class, although one boy asked him to give an example of his use of "poetic license." But for the last twenty minutes of class, the students are free to browse for books. Ashley was immediately surrounded by students and peppered with questions.

Christopher Paul Curtis arrives tonight. I am back at the Muthaiga Club sitting outside under an umbrella at a table on the lawn. The Muthaiga Club was built by the British colonials with pink stucco walls and red tile roofing. They complement the flowering, climbing vines beautifully. I love the ghosts of Karen Blixen, who wrote *Out of Africa,* and Beryl Markham, who wrote *West with the Night,* that linger here. They say that the aviatrix Beryl Markham ended up a lonely old lush hanging out in the Muthaiga bar, avoided by everyone. Oh, I wish she were still sitting in the bar. I would be thrilled and honored to talk to her. There are still elderly British colonial types hanging out here, but for the most part, it is a cosmopolitan crowd.

For those of you who have managed to escape being told the story of why Christopher Paul Curtis is coming, there's no escape. Christopher won the 2000 Newbery Medal Award. I had the great good fortune to serve on the committee that chose his book *Bud, Not Buddy* as the winner. His publisher gave a breakfast for members of the Newbery Committee so that we could meet him. I began talking to him while he was autographing books, and I told him that I appreciated seeing Ashley Bryan's name in his acknowledgments. I went on to tell him that Ashley was coming to Africa with me this year. Christopher looked up and exclaimed, "I want to go to Africa with Ashley!"

Indeed, he is almost here. Ashley did not come with us to meet Christopher because he is at Mount Kenya Academy teaching my classes. (My students are not going to want me to come back after experiencing Ashley Bryan for a few sessions.)

Christopher's wife, Kay, and daughter, Cydney, are also coming toward the end of the month. Mary Evelyn, my daughter, and Scott Hollowell, her fiancé, arrive on Sunday night. They are going on safari, so Charles will not have to set what he calls "The Nairobi Shuttle" into motion for them. They will have a van and driver. They will spend Tuesday, June 12, at Mount Kenya Academy, so we will be a merry band. I will be so glad to see Mary Evelyn. The trouble with having friends and family on opposite sides of the world is that one is always missing those who are opposite. Charity's son, Tony, and his wife, Josephine, live in San Francisco. Their baby girl, Charity's first grandchild, has just been born—Kui (pronounced "Coy.") We have seen pictures of her with her mother, but Charity is also suffering from "Opposite-Side-of-the World Syndrome."

June 16, 2001

Charity's father's funeral was held yesterday. The authors, Ashley Bryan and Christopher Paul Curtis, are teaching at school. Charity's daughter, Wandia, flew in from the U.K. Betty, the other daughter who works in Nairobi, is also here, but son Tony and his wife, who live in San Francisco, are unable to attend.

The funeral was *huge*. The Tumutumu Presbyterian Church was totally packed with people seated on the ground outside. Charity's father, Francis Kiburu, was an elder of the East African Presbyterian Church there. The service was in Kikuyu. The hymns were in Kikuyu but were printed in the program, so I was able to follow along. It was definitely African singing. "Jesus" is sung as "Yesu."

Charity gave a speech, which must have been difficult. It was in Kikuyu, and as I sat there listening to my friend's voice rising and falling, I knew she was speaking of the death of a good father. One story I was told about her father is enlightening. When she was a little girl, he discovered that Charity and her sister were leaving home and playing outside all day instead of walking to school together. When their father learned this, he sent them both to different schools so that they were no longer walking together.

Her father, who was a Kikuyu chief, was born in 1900. After the service, the large congregation departed for the gravesite at his home. Some drove but most walked. Charity's father was buried beside her mother at a beautiful, terraced site on his own property. People stood on grassy, wide terraces like an amphitheater overlooking the gravesite singing African hymns the entire time the grave was being filled in. I stood for a long time looking at the trees and blue sky and listening to hundreds of African voices flowing from one hymn into another. It was absolutely beautiful and unhurried. Our culture is so hurried. We would never take the time for a gravesite service as meaningful as this. Our cultures are different, and the African ways are not our ways, but our ways are often not best.

Mary Evelyn and Scott met me at school after they had spent the night at The Ark, the animal viewing hotel in the Aberdare National Forest. They were there with Ashley Bryan and Christopher Paul Curtis. Mary Evelyn and Scott were on the way to Mount Kenya Safari Club, but they were taking me to the Whitfields' house in Nanyuki first. We all had lunch and then went on a successful "monkey walk" in the forest.

Afterwards, Mary Evelyn and Scott's van got stuck in the mud. Scott and their driver walked back to the house for help while Mary Evelyn guarded the van. Much pushing and shoving and commotion ensued as people arrived to help. Randy finally had to bring the pickup and a rope. After a couple of attempts, the rope broke. Randy dryly observed, "I think it would help if there were more people pushing and fewer people watching." As a professional watcher with a sore arm, I was shamed into pushing with my one good arm. That obviously turned the tide, as my one shove worked. I told Scott that you haven't really been to Africa until you've been stuck in the mud.

Ashley and Christopher have taken Mount Kenya Academy by storm. They move around in clumps, like man-shaped magnets with children stuck to them. Standard Eight is doing a mural all across the back of their classroom called "Ashley Bryan in Africa." I don't want to ruin the surprise, but Christopher will find himself depicted as a warrior.

Inspired by Ashley, the children are reciting poetry all over the campus. They immediately memorize the poems that he recites. He even bumps into children at the Outspan who instantly start reciting "My People" by Langston Hughes.

Christopher has students all completely enamored, as his way of communicating is by joking and teasing—not just a little—but through total immersion. I have lost my constituency. I was reading a story about a teacher to the little Standard Ones. I paused and asked, "Who wants to be a teacher?" Blank looks—no hands raised. "Who wants to be an author?" Every hand waving.

June 22, 2001

My young pastor, Caroline Kelly, came to Kenya. Her father, Dr. Thad Kelly, and her mother, Carolyn, have been here since March. Her father is serving as a volunteer doctor at Chogoria Hospital in Meru District. Caroline is to preach both services at the PCEA Chogoria Church. The early service is in English, but the 11:00 service, which is in Kikuyu, will be translated as Caroline speaks—an experience for all concerned. Caroline's sister, Mary Sydney, is also here. The whole family is now on safari. Caroline and her father came by school for a tour, and then I joined them for a drive to the

Aberdare Country Club for lunch and then a bus ride for an evening of animal viewing at The Ark.

People stay inside The Ark and peer out at the animals that visit the water hole and salt lick. Many animals visited—mostly crabby buffaloes—but also a smattering of elephants (if elephants can be said to smatter). The highlight came at 2:00 in the morning.

The buzzer sounded, scaring everyone out of their sleep and wits, to see the rhino. It was a mother with her baby and the baby's big brother. The baby lay down in the mud and nursed his mother and then continued lying in the mud—seemingly content and comfortable.

July 9, 2001

I'm at Mountain Lodge again in the Mount Kenya National Forest peering out at the bushbucks, large, lovely gray creatures of the antelope family, gathered at the water hole. There are tons of Cape buffalo (literally) in the forest. They hang out here regularly, yet hold no charm. Ah, but the elephants. They love this water hole. They have a large number of baby elephants who are enchanting to watch. There are two large rough stones, and a couple of elephants backed up to them and gave their rear ends a rasping scratch. One elephant laboriously straddled one and rocked back and forth, scratching her vast tummy. When she was satisfied, she moved away with a loud sigh.

A dove flew into the window and broke its neck. A gray

monkey with cream-colored eyebrows, ear rims, and ruff, saw the dove, grabbed it up, scampered up to the top of the building, and began plucking the feathers. A smaller monkey, not big enough to steal this windfall, sat looking longingly at this feast. Lo and behold, while he was watching, another dove killed itself by flying slap into the window. The smaller monkey grabbed it and clambered up and sat beside the bigger monkey. They plucked their doves so expertly that it makes me believe that this is not an uncommon occurrence. I have never seen such a cloud of feathers.

Yesterday afternoon, on the nature walk, I learned valuable information. I can readily identify elephant poop because nine years ago I spent a week slogging through elephant poop while hiking across the Aberdares. Now, I can also recognize rhino poop, buffalo poop, and elephant urine.

There were six wild ducklings paddling frantically around in the water hole—little scraps of life. They seemed to be missing their mother, who was nowhere to be seen. I began to worry about them, but she reappeared and called them out of the water. Then Papa appeared and off they went, with Mama leading, quacking loudly, and Papa guarding the rear. I wonder where they can go safely in this forest where humans are guarded with guns. (I didn't have time to worry about the doves, because they slammed into the window so quickly one after the other, but I did ponder the fact that doves mate for life.) It is a privilege to see animals where they are free and belong only to themselves.

Scott Hawkins and Sarah Hawkins at Kichwa Tembo tented camp

CHAPTER SIX
2002

May 5, 2002

This year, we reversed the schedule and went on safari first. Scott Hawkins, his daughter Sarah, Westminster teacher Woodrow Barnes, and I arrived in Nairobi on Friday night. Yesterday morning, we flew to Masai Mara and were taken to the tented camp, Kichwa Tembo. I have my own tent with a stone-floored bathroom in the back. This is the rainy season, and the sound of the rain hitting the canvas roof is a cozy sound that reminds me of my childhood camps. Back then, however, I didn't have to zip the front and bottom of the tent entrance and tie the zippers together to keep out the baboons. The baboons know how to unzip, but they don't know how to untie...yet.

The camp itself is surrounded by an electric fence to keep out the large dangerous animals. The smaller animals hang out inside the fence where they have learned they are safe. There is a large group of banded mongoose—slim brown animals the size of small, elongated cats with white stripes across their backs—that weave in and out of the bushes in camp. They dig around on the green lawn. I assumed that they were eating a little salad until a guide told me that they are eating insects. They sit up on their hind legs, fold their paws across their stomachs, and peer around every few minutes. Their babies, however, are the size of mice. One baby couldn't keep up with his group, so his mama picked him up by the scruff of his neck and carried him. He went limp like other little mammals, and away they went. The mongoose eat snakes, so they are very welcome in camp.

Warthogs are another group that enjoy the protection of the electric fence. They crawl under the fence and lounge around all over the camp. They take frequent naps. I had three in front of my tent with the middle warthog in the throes of a complicated nightmare. I kept suggesting to his companions that they wake up the noisy sleeper—but they were uncaring pigs.

Warthogs are the ugly, gray cousins of the domesticated pigs, but they have an intelligent gleam in their beady black eyes, and they have a certain charm. They even stretch out beside the open-air dining patio. At dinner, I was examining two right outside the patio and making some comment about warthogs, when Scott called them "resort-hogs." We all fell about laughing, and I complimented him on a great line. Fortunately, he has a daughter along to keep him humble.

Sunday morning, we left camp at 5:30 to fly in a balloon across the Mara. The balloons are huge and their baskets hold up to twelve people. There were ten people in our basket, including the pilot—a young woman in uniform complete with epaulets on her shoulders—and her copilot. I was in a corner where I had an unobstructed view. There was no wind, so we lifted off. We were floating away gently when I had a totally unique experience. All of my life, birdsong has come down to me from the treetops. Because balloons are silent, as we floated away, all of the copious bird songs were beneath our feet.

Just in case you were wondering, here's how the hippopotamus sleeps. They graze on land all night, so by early morning they are all tuckered out and tucked in. They sleep in rows with their bodies in the water and their heads pillowed on the riverbank—except for the baby, who was using her mother's body for a pillow.

Surely, balloon travel has to be the most delightful on our planet—quiet, gentle, offering panoramic views of the Rift Valley—provided you don't care where you are going and are being chased by trucks loaded with breakfast.

Although our pilots would never admit it, and everyone acted like the landing was perfectly normal, I don't think it was. The copilot jumped out and went running with a long rope attached to the top of the balloon to pull it quickly to the side so it wouldn't settle down on top of us and the hot burners. They were turned off but still blazingly hot.

Mr. Copilot was not strong and swift enough, and the balloon started settling down over us. The pilot jumped up and was using her arms around the burners to keep the balloon's fabric from touching the burners. It only lasted a minute while the balloon was pulled all the way to the side, and we all clambered out, but our young pilot was an unsung hero. Scott asked us later if we had noticed her singed eyelashes. They had probably gotten singed when she jumped over the burners.

We saw several lilac-breasted rollers—birds so beautifully colored, with turquoise under their wings, that one can hardly believe they are real. Scott took some excellent pictures of them and other Mara wonders.

May 9, 2002

Hawkins Hall, a wonderful new building given by the Hawkins family, has now been dedicated. It has been built at the end of the two parallel classroom buildings, connecting all three on the second floor by balconies that serve as hallways. On the bottom floor is the school auditorium, which slants steeply downward so that all of the children can see over the heads of the students in front of them. During the dedication ceremony, I was in the front row and turned around, and I could literally see every face.

Scott Hawkins declined speeches and asked for a singing ceremony—a participatory, celebratory occasion. Woodrow Barnes, the visiting Westminster teacher, gave the opening prayer, which led into a torrent of songs, poems, dances, and a very professional production of "The Little Red Hen." Both Sarah and Scott gave brief talks, not speeches. As the whole festive event was being videotaped, Scott had the children wave and shout, "Hello!" to Susan and Carter Hawkins. They had remained in Atlanta because of Westminster's baseball schedule—not to mention Carter's final classes leading up to exams. They were sorely missed, but the children, who had all been wanting to wave at the camera anyway, participated with great enthusiasm.

The top floor of Hawkins Hall consists of offices on one end and a computer room in the middle with computers donated by the Coca-Cola Company. Last year, Cindy Candler brought Nancy Rigby, who promptly hauled us into the office of Bill Egby, the head of the Coca-Cola Company for East and South Africa. This visit, which introduced Mount Kenya Academy to them, came to fruition with a well-equipped computer lab.

The remaining part of the top floor consists of a large, airy, book-filled room (the best kind of room) which has now been officially dedicated as the Kemie Nix Library.

One corner of this room, covered by a large rug and holding the extensive picture book collection, is called the Shirley Whitfield Corner complete with a marble plaque. It is an inviting area in which to sit or lie and read. Outside the library door is another plaque. Please indulge me while I reveal the dedication:

KEMIE NIX LIBRARY
THIS LIBRARY IS GIVEN TO
HONOR THE WORK OF KEMIE NIX
IN PROVIDING LITERATURE TO
CHILDREN AROUND THE WORLD.
OCTOBER 31, 2001

Unveiling this plaque was one of the most touching moments of my life. If you note the day on the plaque, that is the date that the large group organized by Cindy Candler *should* have been here. The actual date of the dedication occurred seven months later. The original planned date of dedicating Hawkins Hall was canceled due to the attacks on the United States on September 11, 2001. This building has allowed all the crowded areas of the school to spread out. Now we all have breathing room. It has become an integral part of the school landscape, and I can no longer remember the school's appearance before Hawkins Hall.

The rainy season has arrived, and it is quite cool. We are all slogging around in the rain. Suzanne and Randy, whose home is in a remote area, ventured out for the dedication, but when they didn't arrive back at their home, their friends started worrying. It turned out that their vehicle got thoroughly stuck in the mud on their way home. They finally slogged through the mud on foot to get home. I think they are socked in for the entire season.

Sarah and Scott will spend tomorrow at school, they will go to the Mount Kenya Safari Club for the night, and then they will start home on Saturday. The week has flown by. We have had so many high spots with them and the children that normal life will seem quite dreary. (Well, not quite—Mount Kenya Academy is many things, but dreary has never been one of them.)

May 10, 2002

Everyone is hoping and planning for a Senior School. A very young-looking architect, Freddie, brought a set of plans, and had a meeting with Scott, Sarah, Charity, Charles, and me. I had a set of plans in front of me and tried to keep up with the conversation. I thoroughly enjoyed listening to Scott, a developer, ask probing questions.

After going over the plans, we rode the bus around the corner to the paved road. Mount Kenya Academy's dirt road is full of mud, holes, and puddles. We then walked up a slight slope into a coffee plantation, where a neighbor of the school was willing to sell land in five-acre increments.

The land is flat, square, and slap across from the entrance to Mount Kenya Academy. For the land to become available right across from school is providential. Charity and Charles had worked to acquire several locations close to school, even though one was an unusual shape, but it had never worked out. Then a member of the Parents' Committee discovered this neighbor was willing to sell. Charles persuaded the owner, who had another buyer, to wait seven months until Scott got here and could peruse it.

We all went tromping around in the mud. I was with Charity and Sarah and said, "Just think, we are walking on the future."

Sarah said, "That sounds just like a Kemie statement."

Scott, Charles, the grumpy owner, and Freddie walked between the coffee plants to see how the property connected with the current school. When they returned Scott announced, "Well, we just bought ten acres for the Senior School." Later, I found Charity crying alone in her office. She said that Scott had told her that he was going to send her a large check. She is supposed to pay a forty percent down payment on the land and keep the rest in a bank account. The economy here is wretched, and Charity had to send away a very bright girl because she couldn't subsidize any more students. She was financially stretched to the limit. After telling me through her tears that she couldn't believe that anyone could be so generous, she added, "The first thing I am going to do is call those parents and tell them to send their girl right back."

May 16, 2002

We went to the Nyamachaki Presbyterian Church in Nyeri on Sunday. I was reluctant to go, not because I don't thoroughly appreciate it, but because it is so crowded and I am always squashed. The Presbyterian Church East Africa is growing at such a rapid rate that every church service is packed. Last time I attended, I literally had a woman squashed under my arm. (I guess I should be grateful that it was a woman.) Charity said we would sit in one of the chairs in the aisle. That's exactly what we did, and instead of moving over when the usher motioned for me to do so, I clung to my perch and made the other attendees climb over me.

The pace of life in the United States is so fast that I feel sure it is not good for us, but the pace here is at the other end of the spectrum. When I come to Africa, it usually takes me a couple of weeks to slow down. (Charles was complaining to me this morning about trying to conduct business in Africa with everything so slow.) The church service lasted over two hours with people drifting in for at least the first hour and a half. It reminded me of the occasion at Central Presbyterian Church in Atlanta when the African-American guest minister told the mostly white congregation, "You white folks don't know that the Holy Spirit doesn't even show up until 12:30."

The church music is wonderful. It is a combination of "golden oldies" and African hymns sung in either Kikuyu or Kiswahili. I'm not sure which. I'm usually able to sing along because the leaders use the call-and-response method. This seems to be how most African songs are sung, and perhaps it traces back to pre-literate times. I haven't been to the Sunday service in Grace Chapel (the school chapel) yet. I look forward to it because all of the children, from the youngest to the eldest, take turns singing—and I am not squashed.

On Tuesday I went to Nairobi, and Michael, the Mwangis' driver, drove me. Nairobi is not my favorite place, and the traffic is horrendous. I am comfortable with Michael though. He is not only smart; he is street-smart. He told me that he had lived in Nairobi for seven years. We went to pick up Linda Thompson at the airport. Linda is assistant director of the children's department of the main branch of the Atlanta Public Library. She is staying at Mount Kenya

Academy in the guest cottage for about three weeks to help sort out the library and to put the books into a computer program. Because her plane didn't arrive until late, we were spending the night at the Norfolk Hotel. When I checked in before going to the airport, the receptionist told me that we were staying in the "Ernest Hemingway Suite." I apparently looked appalled because she added the magic words, "At no extra cost, of course." We were then free to enjoy the luxury.

We are working to put all of the books in proper order via the Dewey Decimal system. Many of the books have come from the Westminster Elementary Library over the years. I'll open a book, and it will have a bookplate "Presented by Robin Robinson '74" or "Presented by Mary Evelyn Nix '76." Other books say, "Presented in loving memory of Scott Blair Bollinger and Raymond Carl Marine." Sarah Hawkins and her friend Anne Stephens gave many new books to the library when Sarah came to dedicate Hawkins Hall. Every book has a bookplate honoring someone important in their growing-up years—usually a teacher from the Westminster of my era. It is like looking at a scrapbook.

The library is getting a proper reorganization. Linda and I are pulling books off the shelves and alphabetizing them until we are both exhausted and dizzy. I didn't realize I was so weak on the alphabet until I spent days thinking about it—and it was one of the very first things I learned at school.

June 21, 2002

No one can control reactions to actions. The September 11 terrorists wanted to sow only terror. John and I were originally scheduled to come last October with the group Cindy Candler had organized. That trip was postponed because of the attack and broke into a May group and a July group. I ended up coming with Sarah and Scott Hawkins in May for the dedication of Hawkins Hall. Because John was coming with the July group, I decided to stay and teach until then. Ashley Bryan was invited to come in that interim, and he arrived a week ago for the last two weeks of June. Many Kenyan children got the pleasure of knowing Ashley, a totally positive experience for them, as a result of all the schedule changes wrought by the terrorists.

We have filled the Shirley Whitfield Corner with Ashley's numerous and beautiful books. The classes sit on the rug at his feet, and they can see his books displayed face out on the bookshelf—including a large new book designed for teachers of creative writing that has a profile portrait of Ashley on its cover. This colorful display lends Ashley the glamor of a movie star.

Ashley's specialty is poetry recitation with wonderful expressiveness and considerable waving of arms and hands. The children are entranced and copy every hand motion, and they are able to mimic every syllable. The result is everyone reciting poetry—especially on the playground. Ashley does recite quieter poems, but the children love the one that Ashley says is the loudest poem in the world: "Baby" by Langston Hughes.

The children go around shouting, "ALBERT, DON'T YOU PLAY IN THAT ROAD!" They are also inordinately fond of "Tickled Pickles Don't Smile" by Nikki Giovanni. When I see and hear their joy in poetry and the presence of Ashley, I think, "Take *that,* You Terrorists."

Yesterday, we went to one of the government schools, Muruguru, and those children also gazed at Ashley with bright eyes and considerable amazement. Linda Thompson brought colorful bookmarks made from Ashley's books, which we laminated for permanence, and Betty Dodds patiently cut out and placed them in packets of a hundred. Not knowing how many children attended Muruguru, I took a thousand bookmarks because I didn't want anyone to be left out. We passed out the bookmarks to reaching hands, and all one thousand evaporated. As we were leaving, I asked the deputy head how many children attended Muruguru, and he said, "Four hundred."

I haven't seen any wild animals recently, except for the large monkey loping across Charity's lawn, but there are domestic animals and chickens galore. As the chickens are all free range, I don't see how anyone manages to capture one to put in the pot. They are all wild and overwrought—at least as they scatter from traffic. The goats and sheep graze along the roadside and are forever deciding that the grass is greener on the other side. They wander across the road at whim. I used to worry about them, but it proved to be wasted concern. I never saw a squashed or injured goat—until today. As we drove home, there was a coal black nanny goat hobbling along with a long white cast on her leg. Considering she was hobbling *in* the traffic, she was obviously one of the dimmer of her species.

June 27, 2002

There is a market on Tuesday, Thursday, and Saturday on the other side of the railroad as you turn down the Mwangis' long driveway. It is the oldest type of market in the world, with produce piled on cloths on the ground. The modern touch is that the ground is covered with plastic trash the next morning. Obviously suffering from a plastic deficiency, the goats eat the plastic, and the ground is clear by the time we return in the evening. They eat the paper too—except for the goat that I saw munching on a discarded corn cob.

Out of my office window (borrowed from Charles), I can see Nyeri Hill, for which the town is named. On Saturday, the scouts were leaving on the school bus to climb Nyeri Hill. One of the songs the children sing in assembly contains the line, "If you can't climb a mountain, then climb a hill..." Inspired by the song and urged on by the scouts, I climbed aboard to go with them. Rebekah Shaffer, our chaplain intern from Columbia Theological Seminary in Decatur, Georgia, was already aboard.

Nyeri Hill isn't. We climbed and climbed—with the girls and boys scampering ahead and the adults shouting, "Wait,

wait!" periodically and fruitlessly. I was finally reduced to asking, "How much further?" To which the cheerful reply was always, "Not much further!"

When we finally reached the top, the keepers of the mobile phone tower wouldn't open the gate for the scouts to climb the last hundred yards or so. Their reasoning, despite pleas, was that Rebekah, a young chaplain, and I, an old lady, were deemed too dangerous.

Last time I went to Nairobi with Charity, we ate lunch at the home of Janice Nga'ng'a, a friend of hers who owns a tea plantation. After the usual huge meal that Kenyans consider hospitable, we rolled out to learn about tea from the foreman, who knows everything there is to know about tea. We learned how new plants are grown—break off a branch, stick it in the ground, and keep it moist and warm; how tea is picked—two leaves and a bud from the top of a tea bush pruned to waist height. We then took a long walk, learning how to prune and sampling the taste of a tea leaf. I can report that it tasted exactly like a leaf. Kenyan tea is so good that Charity won't travel without a personal hoard. (Kenyans in foreign climes seem to pine for their own tea.)

It was Ashley Bryan's last day. He has been here for two weeks that have sped by. He truly is the Pied Piper. The children adore him and mimic him. He has everyone reciting poetry, and he leads the children in and out and around the bookshelves in the library with everyone reciting "Things" by Eloise Greenfield in loud voices—accompanied by much laughter. On Tuesday, we jounced on over to check on what has become known as "Ashley's Water Project" at Kiboya Primary School. Suzanne was our skillful driver, and she pointed out the deadly looking green stream where the children had previously been collecting their water in cans. With the supervision by Charles and the funding by Ashley, two concrete foundations have been laid, and two huge, hideous black plastic tanks have been trucked in from Nairobi. Gutters have also been added to the tin roofs to collect the rainwater so the children will have clean water to drink. There was dancing, singing, and poetry-reciting in honor of two ugly but precious water tanks.

July 4, 2002

When Children's Literature for Children built a library for Chania—a primary school across from Mount Kenya Academy—with contributions from Frances and Ernest Arnold, they named the library after them. Now their granddaughter, Joanna Arnold, is in Kenya working over the summer in Nairobi for a nonprofit. She came up to Nyeri to spend the weekend, and her visit overlapped with Ashley Bryan's last weekend here. Not only did she get to attend one of his classes with the children, she spent the night with Rebekah Shaffer, the chaplain intern. Joanna waxed eloquent about the very ordinary bath in the guest house, which indicated her standard of living in Nairobi. I took both her and Ashley to Mountain Lodge before sending them back to Nairobi with Michael on "The Nairobi Shuttle."

I'm just sorry that Joanna won't be here to meet Dot MacFarlane and Judy Marine. Dot and her husband Ian are touring Africa, ending here for the dedication of the combined chaplain's house and guest house. The name of these two buildings together is the Westminster House, also given by Cindy Candler. Judy Marine is coming with Cindy's group on the twentieth. The Westminster House is to be dedicated in honor of Randy and Suzanne Whitfield.

July 30, 2002

After Cindy arrived with an illustrious group of people representing Westminster and First Presbyterian, only Bill Clarkson (the president of The Westminster Schools), George Wirth (the pastor of First Presbyterian), and last but not least John Nix, were arriving late, to stay only a few days for the dedication. Cindy, Charity, and I set off on "The Nairobi Shuttle" to pick up these gentlemen at 11:00 PM when the KLM flight from Amsterdam arrived. We waited patiently, peering through the glass doors into the baggage-retrieval and customs-check room—and waited and waited. They never appeared. Completely baffled, we returned to the Muthaiga Club for the brief remainder of the night. In the morning, we returned to the airport for the next plane arrival from Europe. The men finally arrived, laughing about their misadventures with missed connections and hurried plane switches that left no time to call and warn us that they wouldn't be on the KLM flight.

Members of the "Dedication of Westminster House" group set off on various safaris in the interim. John and I joined Florida and Doug Ellis and their daughter Florida Huff, Dot, Ian, Judy, and others on a trip to the Mount Kenya Safari Club—always a treat. I was busy trying to persuade everyone to join me the next day for a brief visit to Burgeret Primary School, which was close to the main road.

As Doug and the two Floridas were leaving the Mount Kenya Safari Club, the driver of their van spied an elephant close to the road. Young Florida climbed out to get a better picture of the elephant—which resulted in an elephant emergency. Master Elephant objected to having a flash bulb go off during this portrait session and charged. While charging elephants are famous for speed, young Florida managed to hastily jump back into the van, which safely sped away.

Some members of the group did stop and visit Burgeret Primary School, including the Ellis family, Dot and Ian, and Judy Marine. I was eager for people to visit one of the primary schools where Children's Literature for Children is working. They did see large classes of smiling children bedazzled by visitors.

The dedication was a thorough success with a few brief speeches and much singing. Suzanne and Randy unveiled the plaque in their honor. The plaque is inscribed with these words:

WESTMINSTER HOUSE
GIVEN TO THE GLORY OF GOD
AND IN HONOR OF
SUZANNE AND RANDOLPH WHITFIELD
BY CINDY CANDLER
FIRST PRESBYTERIAN CHURCH OF ATLANTA
DEDICATED JULY 21, 2002

Instead of staying at Outspan as usual, the group stayed at the Aberdare Country Club with a visit to The Ark, that hotel's outpost in the Aberdares. (At the club, John and I received a call from our son reporting that our beloved little terrier, Lindsey, had been killed by a bigger dog at the kennel where John had left our two little dogs while he came to Kenya.)

We continued on to the Masai Mara, and I found myself on an amazing animal drive with two of my dearest friends, Judy Marine and Dot MacFarlane. Being together in the Mara has to be one of the most astonishing highlights of friendships cemented by working together at Westminster. After having visited Burgeret, and knowing my loosey-goosey modes of operation, Dot decided that Children's Literature for Children needed to be taken in hand. Unbeknownst to me (depriving themselves of my helpful suggestions), she and Judy had a long afternoon's talk in the lounge of the Lodge. Neither of them wanted to be the president, so they agreed to be co-presidents. Then they informed me. This really was another critical junction, as CLC had outgrown my ability to manage it alone. Knowing that Dot had keen business acumen, this plan offered assurance that Children's Literature for Children would go forward to flourish instead of to flounder.

First class of Mount Kenya Academy Senior School

CHAPTER SEVEN
2004

January 22, 2004

Because KLM has left Atlanta, the airline has added an extra leg to a trip from Atlanta to Nairobi—Atlanta to Detroit—in the dead of winter. Detroit was totally gray with snow falling hard from a dark sky. I stood at an airport window watching planes take off. With the sound muffled and everything veiled with snow, the planes taking off looked like gray whales rising through a gray sea. Considering the time and expense of de-icing the plane, I can't imagine that adding this new leg is very thrifty. Amsterdam was encrusted with snow, but the last vestiges of winter disappeared when we landed in Nairobi. We rode into town with the cool tropical air flowing into the car window—add the local exhaust, and I rejoiced at returning.

Back in the United States, John and I are the guardians of one of my Mount Kenya Academy students, Krystle Kabare.

She has a scholarship to Rabun Gap–Nacoochie School in north Georgia, thanks to the good offices of George Wirth, pastor of First Presbyterian Church, who arranged it.

In August a couple of years ago, I had an empty nest. September showed a quick reversal. Suddenly, I found myself buying ballet slippers and joining the Parent-Teacher Association. Krystle, when asked if she knew anyone in the United States, had replied, "I know my teacher, Mrs. Nix."

Krystle is now a junior honor student at Rabun Gap–Nacoochie School, a boarding school. Her mother met me at the airport. I regretted that it was I and not Krystle. I'm sure Florence did too, but she welcomed me with the usual generous Kenyan hospitality. Charles Mwangi also came to the airport to help with luggage. He has welcomed me patiently as a houseguest many times over the years.

After my first night under mosquito netting in a couple of years, we set off for Nyeri.

The rainy season is supposedly over. Hardly. Kenya has had great trouble with flooding, but the countryside is beautiful and green, with lots of healthy-looking sheep and goats wandering everywhere. (Suzanne taught me how to tell the difference: "Tail up, goat. Tail down, sheep.")

The walking population along the roadsides can be indicative of social change. When I first started coming to Kenya in 1990, almost every walking woman had a baby on her back. Then birth control became available to the general population, and the babies disappeared—or, rather, grew up. In previous visits, during the time when parents had to pay for primary education, there were children, whose parents couldn't afford school fees, all over the place, walking, herding—carrying stuff, if they were girls. When Mwai Kibaki, the newly elected president of Kenya, decreed that primary education was free, the children, except for preschoolers, also disappeared from the roadside. Traveling in the morning from Nairobi to Nyeri, commenting on the lack of children, Charles told me that it is now the law that children have to be in school, or the parents get taken to court. That is a major, wonderful change.

I couldn't wait to see Mount Kenya Academy Senior School, so we went right there with the boxes of school supplies that had miraculously made it from Atlanta through Detroit and Amsterdam to Nairobi with my luggage. (Just as everywhere else, security was very tight and very crabby at Jomo Kenyatta Airport in Nairobi.)

We drove up a long driveway to a spectacular new school. Scott Hawkins decreed that the school *had* to be completed in one year. It was not there when I left in 2002, and—VOILÀ—there it was in January of 2004 with green fields and buildings sparkling clean for Opening Day.

Mount Kenya Academy had been advertising widely to attract students for the first class, Form One, of the Senior School. One of the unforeseen consequences is that enrollment in the Junior School has burgeoned, with students whose parents are planning ahead. While this was a welcome development, Charity was fretting because only six students were showing up for the first day. Scott said not to worry if we started with only six—it was a start.

We went back to school on Tuesday morning, and here were five young men in their new uniforms—khaki trousers, white shirts, blue-and-white checked ties, and navy V-necked sweaters—looking very handsome. Along came Charlotte, our lone girl, in her khaki skirt, towering over the boys. They lined up to have their pictures taken for posterity, and they were picking threads off their new clothes and straightening their ties, justifiably proud of themselves.

Now it is Thursday of the first week, and we are already up to eighteen students. It is a delight to have everything new and fresh at the same time. I've been working and teaching in the new library—minus books—and teaching in the Junior School. I have now taught all levels from kindergarten through high school. They are all just people—some just have more teeth than others.

This afternoon, three large, chunky young men burst into Charity's office at the Junior School, startling her badly. The ringleader said, "Mrs. Mwangi, I want you to know that I am now a grown man, and I still dream about Mount Kenya Academy!"

January 29, 2004

I have once again bumped Charles out of his office on the second floor of Hawkins Hall at the Junior School. I can look out the windows over the green landscape to Nyeri Hill in the foreground with the blue ridge of the Aberdare Mountains in the background. The windows are open without screens, and the air is fresh and pure. The noises that drift in the windows are birds chirping, cows mooing, and children laughing. It is strange never to hear an airplane, but I haven't heard one since I staggered off of one in Nairobi.

The daytime is warm, and the children wear white shorts and salmon pink, short-sleeved T-shirts when they are playing outside.

I am enjoying teaching my classes. The joys of being a book teacher have proved to be the same wherever I have found myself. All one really needs are actual books, which can be found wherever a library exists. First and foremost, the book teacher indicates to the students that the reading of books is a requirement, but oh, such a pleasant one. They can choose what books they want to read. Class time is spent sharing books in whatever manifestation encourages interaction with books. For example, in order to give the older students an excuse to peruse and enjoy picture books, the teacher can show several illustrations from diverse artists to introduce different styles and perspectives. Then students can be turned loose in the picture book section to find examples on their own. Soon they lose their sense of their superior age and sophistication, and find themselves laughing and sharing their discoveries with one another.

The aspect of teaching books that I relish the most is helping with book selection during the last part of the class.

Students must be given ample time, either alone or with help from each other or the teacher, to look for the next book they want to read. I always enjoy their new requests as the students' special interests expand and develop. One bright-eyed child who was beginning to enjoy fairy tales said, "I want another mean, cruel book!"

Because I teach all the children in the school, I require the children to sit in the same place every class to facilitate learning their names. The little ones in Standards One, Two, and Three sit on the library rug in rows. The individuality of every person, even a very small person, never ceases to amaze me. You can discern this in short order. I had placed nametags in rows on the rug where I wanted the Standard Ones to sit. Eve, no bigger than a minute, picked up her nametag with her name on it from the back row and moved it to the front and stated, "I'm going to sit in the front row."

Leo and Diane Dillon are two wonderful illustrators who serve on the Advisory Board of Children's Literature for Children. They once said something that I have been pondering ever since. One of them said, "Light is light," and the implication was that the quality of light is the same no matter where you are. Here we are seven thousand feet high on the equator—so the quality of light seems unusually radiant to my eyes. To those of us used to changing amounts of daylight, I wonder how a consistent twelve hours of sunlight and twelve hours of darkness all the time affects the personality—positively, I would imagine. One friend whose children grew up in Kenya had a son who went off to boarding school in England. He called his mother and said he wanted to come home, "Because no one is happy here." The quality of happiness in Kenyans that he missed probably is not due soley to the amount of light, but when I wake up to fresh, sparkling, bright mornings, I can't help but feel happy.

Kenya got rid of the dictator Moi last January. Even in just a year, good changes have occurred. On the Kiganjo-Nanyuki road, just outside of Kiganjo, a huge mill and a large dairy creamery (called the "National Creamery") have been closed as long as I can remember. They are both back in business. Charles told me that the machinery in both had been maintained even while they were closed. There seems to be hope in the air, and Charity says the economy is slowly improving—despite the fact that the country was robbed by Moi and his cronies. The new government has set out to get the purloined fortunes back from foreign banks. Very smart people are on the money trails, and reading about it in local newspapers is quite interesting. Nairobi is still a "den of thieves," but the government has just raised the salaries of all the police. The most encouraging development is that primary education is now free. The government schools have been overrun as a result. One eighty-four-year-old man showed up in a school uniform at a Standard One class, because he wanted to learn to read. His picture has been in all the papers with all of his little classmates goggling at him. Good for him.

I love seeing Mount Kenya again. Pictures never have the same emotional impact that seeing the living mountain does. I am also terribly saddened by looking at Mount Kenya for the families that lost loved ones in a tragic plane crash last year. Fourteen members of the same extended family, including my student, Bill Love, and members of his immediate family, were killed when their plane crashed into the mountain. This was a devastating blow to many in their respective communities—including Westminster and Trinity Presbyterian Church of Atlanta. Charity also told me of people she knew who had been killed while climbing the mountain. Extremely beautiful but dangerous.

I have always liked donkeys and sympathized with them, as they have not fared well under the domination of humans. Life is not fair even—or maybe especially—if you are an animal. Donkeys will be walking along one side of the road with huge burdens, and the zebras on the other side of the road are totally free. (I have always wanted a baby donkey—considering them the most charming of animals.) This week, I have observed many donkeys that are just wandering around and grazing. I don't know how to account for it, but it seems pleasant for the donkeys. Also, the elephants in the Samaburu desert seemingly subsist on a diet of sticks, while the elephants in the Aberdare Forest live on lush vegetation. Life. Is. Not. Fair.

Ashley Bryan, the beloved friend of us all, arrives tomorrow. Debbie Green, the director of Children's

Literature for Children, arrives on February 5—and so does Kay Curtis, the wife of author Christopher Paul Curtis. We will sally forth to visit schools where CLC has been working. (Debbie will stay with me at Charity's house. Kay will stay at the Outspan, where Ashley is also staying. The staff there knows Ashley well from his many visits, and they enjoy spoiling him.)

Charity and I have already visited Chania, the primary school across the road from the Senior School. This is the school where our students will be involved in community service. Charity is determined that community service, which has not been a strong component of the extended and extensive family-oriented culture of Kenya, will be a strong component of the Senior School. Being family oriented has been a survival mechanism for many generations of Kenyans. (Frequently, upon arriving home from school, we will discover some relative sitting on the sofa waiting to ask Charles for help.) Children's Literature for Children has built a wonderful library at Chania. It is made of stone and is as carefully built as the Senior School itself. The corrugated tin roof also has corrugated plastic panels that let light into the room and serve as skylights. The Frances and Ernest Arnold Library is the largest of the school buildings. This light-filled building has tables, benches, and bookshelves. While not filled with books yet, it is well on its way.

February 6, 2004

An adolescent monkey ran over my shoe—almost. Regarded as pests by the Kenyans, monkeys tend to give wide berth to humans. I don't see them often, so I was delighted to see a troop of small black-faced monkeys. I was at the gate of the Junior School when I saw a monkey scampering down the middle of the dirt road with the branches of nearby trees swaying wildly. Then another monkey ran past. I went out the gate and watched monkeys raining from the trees and running past me down the road. Some mothers had babies clinging to their fur. (Something must have scared them.) They were very fast and cast horrified looks over their shoulders at me. After they disappeared down the road, I turned to go back through the gate, and an alarmed straggler almost ran across my toe. In Atlanta, practically the only sign of wild animals is roadkill. In Kenya, everyone lives much closer to nature, and there is an abundance of animal life everywhere. Most of the wild animals, however, have been driven back into the forest preserves. Charles told me that there were two leopards in the vicinity of the house. When I asked where they were, he waved vaguely in the direction of Mount Kenya. The local herdsmen call them "Mwangi's Leopards," and even tried to make Charles pay for their gobbled sheep. Good luck with that.

While Charity eats fruit in her room every morning, Debbie has joined me in the dining room for breakfast. The eggs we eat are so fresh that we are personally acquainted with the hens. (Back in the United States, we have forgotten the taste of fresh eggs.) We look out the dining room windows at the roses by the front walk. The bougainvillea runs riot everywhere in shades of red, white, pink, and purple. The geraniums by the front door are so massive they have trunks instead of stems. After breakfast, Charity drives us to school, where we enter into the day's activities. The dirt road on the way to school is being resurfaced from huge piles of crushed rocks, making navigation difficult. We saw an old woman laboriously rolling a huge boulder across the road, and men and women were shoveling rocks onto the roadbed by hand. We also saw an old woman bent under a load of logs. These are real people dealing with enormous burdens that you and I will never know. (I like to complain about books being heavy.)

February 15, 2004

After Debbie Green and Kay Curtis arrived, they joined Charity, Ashley, and me in the school van to visit government schools where we have built libraries and/or contributed water tanks. Our first stop was Muruguru Primary School, where the school had set aside a classroom they have kindly named the Kemie Nix Library. A teacher, George Ndirangu, is the librarian. I noticed that he was carrying around two well-worn books: a Bible, and a book about Helen Keller. I asked him about this choice of books, and he told me that his little daughter had been born blind, and that the book about Helen Keller had helped both him and his wife come to terms with her handicap. His child attends the Thika School for the Blind in Thika, a town between Nairobi and Nyeri. (After hearing this story, we want to help that school by providing books in Braille.)

Muruguru has done much with very little. Kay, who is a member of the Windsor, Ontario Rotary Club, believes that she can get that Rotary involved with Muruguru. Kay came loaded with school supplies and small gift packages of toiletries for the older students. This is a growing school of more than four hundred students, and I believe that every one of them ran out to supervise our departure. Some of the smaller students surrounded our school van and told us with big smiles, "Flat tire. Flat tire."

One tiny child kept putting his hand on the right rear tire, telling me it was flat. I examined it and told him confidently, "No, it isn't flat." We departed after an exchange of good will all around, drove out to the main road, and—CLUNK, CLUNK.

We visited eight schools, an exhausting but touching process. Most now have libraries. Ndiriti Primary School has books but no library. Simon Russell is a student at Westminster. For his Eagle Scout Project, he shipped six hundred pounds of processed books to Ndiriti. They are carried around to classrooms in crates. All of the buildings are seemingly made of sticks, and the quadrangle is a sea of mud. Nevertheless, Ndiriti is so strong academically that children come from all over to attend. Some even arrive on the ever-present mode of transportation—small, usually overloaded vans. The smallest children must have been four or five, and they were lined up against a wall in their red uniforms with plastic cups in their hands filled with a milky-looking porridge that had been cooked over an open fire. Thankfully, they had something to fill their stomachs. Not all of the children at all of the schools do.

After we had visited the classrooms, some children led us to a row of chairs placed in the open field behind the school. The honored guests sat facing the students, who performed poems and dances. Once again, the smallest children, looking baffled by the whole experience, were arranged in front. After we clapped loudly, the children came pressing around us and getting in everyone's way as we tried to leave, until a teacher told them that they could have a "sweet" after they got back to their classrooms. The whole crowd immediately ran away toward their classrooms cheering. (Ndiriti gets the next library.)

We next visited Kiboya Primary School, which has been Ashley's special project. (While at Kiboya, one teacher and I were discussing our long acquaintance when she tactfully observed, "You used to be thin. Now you are fat.") The school now has a classroom building, three water tanks, a library, a fence, and a watchman. We went to meet the watchman, who is from a northern tribe. He called to his wife, who was in their small hut, to come out to meet us. The curtain serving as a door was pushed aside, and this exquisitely beautiful woman, who could have graced the cover of *Vogue*, stepped out holding an adorable three-month-old baby on her hip.

That is one thing I have always appreciated about God's world. Beauty and intelligence spring up everywhere. Power and money cannot command them.

After school visits, the "visiting firemen" portion of our group went to Mountain Lodge to spend the night and view the animals. I love Mountain Lodge because you get taken on long nature walks. After being fitted with gum boots, we set off. Everyone has different ideas about what is fun, I suppose, but as we squished off through the mud and elephant poop, with me trying to keep up with the youngsters, I thought, "This is so much fun!"

September 10, 2004

Charity, her daughter Betty, Ashley Bryan, and I are on the plane returning from the huge Johannesburg airport to Nairobi. We left Cape Town at 6:00 this morning—which necessitated getting up at 3:30 AM. Betty, who is extremely competent, herded her sleepy sheep on board for the first leg of the journey and then rounded us up onto the plane for the second leg.

Cape Town was a new wonder to me. The city is lovely. Table Mountain behind the city is breathtaking, and the bay is gorgeous. There are ever-increasing shanty towns outside of the city. The air blowing off the bay keeps more of the dust out of the air than in Nairobi, where the dust can be horrible. (At Olympic Primary School in the Kibera slum where we have built a library, everything is dusty during the dry season—except for the children's shining faces.) In the slums around Cape Town, the views are beautiful and the air is clean. The trains still run out of town around five o'clock carrying workers to the segregated townships. The influences of apartheid remain. Yet, Cape Town reminded me of all the beautiful bay cities of the world without that special African essence, which Nairobi has. It had been driven out of Cape Town. I hope it returns.

We all met in Cape Town because Charity, Ashley, and I were making a presentation at the International Board of Books for Young People World Congress. There were six hundred people from sixty-eight countries there. I would not normally come to Africa twice in one year, but the theme for this congress was "Books for Africa." Children's Literature for Children, through our outreach program, Reader-to-Reader, has sent more children's books to Africa than any other organization. I am aware that the dark side goes along with everything good we try to do. I know that our books are written in English from the United States. All the standardized and critically important tests for individuals to further their education in Kenya are written in English. Teachers and parents want the children to begin reading stories in English as soon as possible for academic reasons. The children just want to read stories. I can only hope that the books we give are exotic and interesting to African children. (The best children's books published in Africa are found in South Africa. My hope for the future is to buy more books from South Africa.)

I knew Children's Literature for Children had to be represented at this congress, and I persuaded Charity and Ashley to appear on the stage with me. Betty, who is an electrical engineer served as one for us—literally. Charity brought a PowerPoint presentation, which Betty supervised. Ashley said that he was so relieved he didn't have to bring slides.

Charity talked about how she developed Mount Kenya Academy and how Reader-to-Reader: Africa started as community outreach from Mount Kenya Academy. I talked about how I invited author Christopher Paul Curtis and author-illustrator Ashley Bryan to come with me to MKA in 2001. We took these two luminaries to visit our library projects at several government schools. Ashley promptly adopted the poorest, and he and Christopher also planned to contribute water tanks to three schools, which they did.

On the stage, Ashley spoke next. He described the water projects that he and the Curtis family had underwritten. The children at Kiboya and two other government schools received two huge black water tanks per school to hold clean rainwater so that the children don't have to carry water from contaminated streams. The tanks have been installed with the supervision of Charles Mwangi and Suzanne Whitfield. Suzanne has also planted trees galore, which have received school water from the water tanks. (The children helped with the tree planting by each bringing a small bag of goat manure to help enrich the soil and serve as a source of merriment.) The barren areas have "greened up" with amazing rapidity.

The PowerPoint presentation showed these transformations. Ashley also told about the new library he has contributed to his special school. The Ashley Bryan Library is the first stone building at a school basically built of sticks.

The most meaningful aspect of our time in Cape Town to me was the visit to Robben Island. The trip on the ferry was long and cold. The prisoners obviously couldn't swim away from the island. We walked through the prison and peered into Mandela's tiny cell, which had contained one human but such a large heart.

We also visited the quarry where prisoners served their "hard labor." As a rock collector with rocks from all over the world, I wanted to get off the bus and "collect" a rock. I wasn't allowed to do so, but I suppose the quarry would disappear if every tourist were allowed to make off with a rock. We saw the large cave used as a latrine, and while we were looking at it, a huge mole snake slithered out to sun itself—or bite foolish rock collectors.

Our guide around the prison was a former prisoner who had been incarcerated from the age of seventeen to twenty-three. He was smiling and friendly. He said that forgiveness was what enabled him to teach others about the history of the prison. Here was a living middle-aged example of forgiveness with smile crinkles around his eyes. Enough forgiveness emerged from this prison to transform a nation.

I wonder what it feels like to be Nelson Mandela. He is a human being with virtues and flaws—but to wake up every morning with that great transforming heart...

September 18, 2004

It's Saturday morning, and I am on the veranda waiting for the van that has collected Ashley from the Outspan. Ashley has just won the Coretta Scott King Award for his wonderful book, *Beautiful Blackbird.* The van is then swinging by school to pick up Vickie and Geoff Ruskin. Vickie is the volunteer librarian who has gotten the libraries of both schools in tip-top shape. Geoff is a retired teacher who has been pitching in and teaching all over the place. We are going to Nanyuki to visit a weaving cooperative. We will stop at the Trout Tree restaurant—one of my favorite restaurants on the planet. (John hosted our church group there last spring.) It consists of large platforms at different levels built into huge trees with the trout farm pools below and the colobus monkeys above. (The platforms have canvas tent tops because of the colobus monkeys.)

The colobus monkeys are not only found at Trout Tree, they are right here at home. They are the large black-and-white monkeys with long fur and elegant white tails. They have white ruffs around their black wizened faces with down-turned mouths, which makes them look like disgruntled old men forced to dress up for the opera. The babies are so exquisite and so light that the branches hardly sway as they leap about. I watched an all-white colobus baby swing over to its mother for a reassuring cuddle before venturing off again. It was so much like a human child that I laughed.

I never tire of the flora and fauna of Kenya, but they

and the people are greatly stressed because the spring rains never came. Weather forecasters predict that the small rains in October will arrive. I pray that they are right. Charity's garden is still beautiful, however. The lovely, long-tailed, black-and-white birds called wagtails strut across the grass doing just that. Perhaps that behavior stirs up insects.

Charity may have some lovely insects in her attic. There has been a mysterious scurrying sound coming from the attic over my bedroom. It sounded like the sound our resident squirrels make at our house in the United States. (The squirrels here are very small, shy creatures, unlike our brisk, confident ones.) Muthoni happened to be with me when the scurrying sound occurred in the attic. I asked her what it was. She replied, "Butterflies. Are you scared?"

"No, not of butterflies."

It shall remain a picturesque mystery.

My favorite Kenyan sound remains the distinctive, long drawn-out cooing of the dove. Ashley and I discovered one in a tree by Charity's front walkway. It continued cooing with its small breast expanding rhythmically. Ashley compared it to the rhythm of a drum.

With the current drought, the elephants are coming out of Mount Kenya National Forest and foraging at night. Charles told me that it is dangerous to go walking at night because of the elephants. I wasn't planning to go walking at night—but lurking elephants and butterflies clinch the deal.

Suzanne Staples planting a tree at Nyeri Primary School with Kay Curtis in the background

CHAPTER EIGHT
2009

January 18, 2009

Kenya is always delightful, but especially in January. I am back on Charity's veranda watching the colobus monkeys frolicking in the tree in the corner of the yard. The monkeys only come on Sundays. There must be too much human activity for them the rest of the week. They only eat the fruit of this particular tree. As they don't bother other crops or fruit, they are allowed to exist. Charles called me to see them and pointed out the "Big Boss" higher in the tree than the others. He was supposedly the guardian of the group, but he was derelict in his duties as he was sound asleep.

There are five of us on this excursion: Ashley Bryan, Kay Curtis, picture book author-illustrator Leslie Tryon, young adult book author Suzanne Staples, and me. Because school has just opened, we decided to go on safari first to give students time to settle into the routine of school.

Off we went to Treetops, where guests can observe animals coming to the water hole. The animals are also drawn to the salty earth, both natural and enhanced by the hotel. After the guests retire, the hotel buzzes the rooms a certain number of times for the various animals, and everyone rushes out to stand around in the chilly air with a bunch of strangers in their pajamas observing whomever has arrived under the spotlights around the water hole. The buzzer sounded for elephants, and we all rushed out. There was an elephant family of six female adults led by a large matriarch and six youngsters. It was a delight watching the young elephants play by wrestling with their trunks. There was a tiny baby who could walk under the adults. Once everyone was occupied drinking and eating delicious dirt, the baby decided to run away. Off she ran as fast as she could into the outer darkness. When her mama realized what was happening, she and an aunt went after her and brought her back. Then once everybody settled back down—*WHOOPS*—off she ran again. The adults went after her again, seemingly good-naturedly. I predict that she is going to grow up to be a handful—or trunkful, as the case may be.

From Treetops, we went to Sweetwater, a tented camp by a small lake populated by a vast array of wildlife. I had never seen a giraffe drink before, and it is a complicated business. First, the giraffe peers around carefully (I assume for predators), then extends one foreleg to the side, then the other. This continues until the legs are widely splayed. Finally the giraffe bends its graceful neck to drink. Giraffes both look and are vulnerable while drinking, but we were told that they only drink once a day. Once, during our visit, the water hole was totally devoid of animals. Apparently, Sir Lion decided he was thirsty and cleared out the neighborhood. I was sorry to have missed him.

There are some gorgeous starlings with purple iridescent backs, low yellow necklaces in front with red breasts beneath. They are called "superb starlings," which they are, but our group could never keep their name straight. Ashley suggested, "splendid sparrows," but that didn't sound right. Finally Leslie suggested, "alliterative starlings," which they became for the remainder of our visit.

I sprinkled some breadcrumbs in front of Suzanne's and my tent. The starlings descended right away and even came close to our feet to retrieve some dropped crumbs. They didn't seem shy, so I began to wonder if they would eat from my hand. The alliterative starlings had fledglings as big as the adults. The fledglings fluttered their wings until their parents fed them (although they were perfectly capable of pecking their own crumbs).

I put crumbs in my hand, rested my hand on the table, and waited quietly. Finally, a brave alliterative starling landed on the table and cautiously approached and pecked a crumb from my hand. When nothing disastrous happened, the others flew over and ate from my hand. One even stepped onto my hand with his prickly, tiny black claws. A fledgling also flew onto the table and fluttered his wings until his parents relented and fed him. He found the whole experience so exhausting that he settled down to rest with his wings splayed right next to my hand. He rested and pooped and rested and pooped.

January 22, 2009

This has been a quick trip. We went to see three schools yesterday, and three today. Plus we have spent time at both the Junior School and the Senior School. On Friday, we went to two schools. We went with a delegation from the Junior School to Nyeri Primary School for the dedication of the Janine and Lloyd Alexander Library. I had told Charity previously that we just wanted to make a "simple visit," and (because Kenyans are so hospitable and prone to "killing the fatted calf" for visitors) to "not make a fuss." Charity relayed that message.

We arrived to sixteen hundred children in chairs on the lawn with parents arrayed under tents around the perimeter. We were seated in the front behind a table covered by a tablecloth with an array of soft drinks at every place. The dignitaries were seated behind us.

First, each one of us planted a tree (mine was a fig tree). Next, some children helped us wash our hands over a basin, and we returned to our seats for the entertainment. There was singing, dancing by the students in multicolored outfits, and flag-raising by scout troops. Next, we were lined up, Suzanne, Leslie, Ashley, Kay, and myself. A darling girl in a blue uniform marched up swinging her elbows and announced loudly to a line of bemused adults that it was time to "inspect the troops." Our leader stepped out smartly with an obedient line of adults trailing behind her. We went up and down rows of uniformed students with serious expressions—except for one of the girls who couldn't help grinning. We returned to our seats for speeches and speeches. Several speakers noted that they now had a library but no books.

Among the polite but bored children, we were amused to see one boy reading his book—the point of the whole event. It started raining, which galvanized the children and gave them a much needed break. They scattered in all directions, holding their chairs over their heads. When it came time for my reply to the festivities, boxes and boxes of books were brought to the front. (Charity had brought the books with us to fill the library.) I tried to be mercifully brief.

We then trooped around to the front of the library for both the ribbon-cutting and the unveiling of the gold plaque reading, "The Janine and Lloyd Alexander Library." It really is a fine library—soon to be filled with books. We were then fed a delicious lunch in a specially decorated hall. If this was Nyeri Primary School's idea of "not making a fuss," I can't imagine what "making a fuss" would entail.

After we left Nyeri Primary School, we headed straight for Muruguru Primary School, which Kay has adopted. The windows and floors are being repaired, and the wretched, muddy quadrangle has been sown with grass that is actually growing. This is just the beginning for Kay. She has enlisted her Rotary in Windsor, Ontario, and soon Muruguru will be much improved. The amount of school supplies that Kay managed to stuff into two duffle bags is staggering.

On and on we jounced over the next few days, visiting schools where we have built libraries. (We are up to nine so far.) Our next library will be built this year at Burgeret Primary School. This library will be the Diana Huss Green Library, after the founder of *Parents' Choice* magazine. Thousands of review copies of books have been given to schools in Kenya through the good offices of Diana.

Both Suzanne Staples and Leslie Tryon are visiting Kenya for the first time. Suzanne has lived all over the world, and she has set several of her books in Pakistan, where she was a reporter. I have admired every one of her books and was eager for the children in Kenya to know her. While the others have been staying at the Outspan Hotel in Nyeri, where Ashley is a great favorite, Suzanne has lived in her own little house on the school campus. This has given the students a real chance to interact with her. We have a good collection of her books in our library, starting with her first book, *Shabanu: Daughter of the Wind,* which is set in the Cholistan Desert of Pakistan. This book burst onto the children's book scene and promptly won a Newbery Honor Award from the American Library Association. I have wanted Suzanne to visit Mount Kenya Academy for years and have delighted in her company. I'm not the only one. One little girl announced that her favorite authors were Enid Blyton (the British author of the Famous Five series) and Suzanne Staples.

In addition to writing and illustrating books starring an illustrious duck named Albert, Leslie is a tap dancer. Much to the delight of Mount Kenya Academy Junior School students, Leslie tap danced for them in assembly. She also gave a tap dancing seminar at the Senior School. Later, a small Standard One boy was observed hopping around outside his classroom—obviously attempting to tap dance.

We also visited Kiboya Primary School, the school that Ashley adopted. Ashley started with water tanks and then he built their first library, the Ashley Bryan Library. He has gradually added buildings. One classroom building was built in Ashley's honor by Alan Stuart of Greenwich, Connecticut. This year, we inspected the second classroom building, built in memory of Ashley's precious sister, Ernestine Bryan Haskins. There is a gold plaque in her honor, which we kept secret from Ashley until he arrived. (Suzanne reported that this plaque was put up just as Ashley was stepping out of the van. Although the cement hadn't had time to harden, the plaque looked as though it had been there forever—which it now will be.) It was also announced that a third classroom building will be constructed, given by Ashley to honor his dear friend, Effie Lee Morris.

This was our last stop on a hectic but delightful visit to Kenyan schools before packing up and heading home. It is always hard to say, "Goodbye."

President Mwai Kibaki with Charles Mwangi

EPILOGUE
2012
Goodbye to Charles

September 5, 2012

Charles Mwangi died.

September 6, 2012

The news of Charles's death flew around the world. Cindy Candler called and said that she wanted to attend the funeral. "What say you?"

September 15, 2012

A grave had been dug in the yard.

A huge tent had been placed in a field between the long driveway and the railroad that is parallel to the Kiganjo-Nanyuki Road. The tent was right outside the fence around the house—the size necessitated by the fact that the entire Mount Kenya Academy Junior and Senior Schools, the community, the churches, family and friends, and the president of Kenya were going to be in attendance. (In the past, going to school necessitated driving more than a kilometer out of the way—up the long driveway, across the intersection, and down the road. Charles had been trying for years to get permission from the government to cut across from the gate, over the railroad tracks, to the main road. The irony is that the road was promptly built when President Kibaki decided to attend the funeral.)

Needing to freshen up before the funeral, I entered the house to head for the bathroom that had been mine on all visits. Lo and behold, a security guard stopped me and said no one was allowed in the house. I asked, "Why ever not?"

Because the president of Kenya was going to enter the house. I pondered this for about two seconds and replied, "I am going to use my *own* bathroom, and you can't stop me."

I note that I wasn't wrestled to the floor.

Later when Kibaki *did* enter the house and talked to the gathered family, Charles's grandchild Little BuBu (pronounced "Bo Bo") accompanied the president of Kenya to the door and graciously invited him to return "any time."

Cindy and I had been asked to make remarks. We were seated in the second row behind members of the immediate family. I was directly across the aisle from President Kibaki's special chair. We were all shooed down a seat so that the president's security guard could sit by me. When I offered to share the words of the hymn, he declined.

As people got up to speak, Charles's three children gave eloquent, touching speeches about their father. Even Charity, who remained a rock of composure for everyone throughout the long funeral, had prepared a tribute. She did not read her speech but stood by her friend, Margaret Githinji, as she read Charity's words. (Later, I was able to put my arm around Charity briefly beside the grave—the point of the whole trip for me.) As other speakers got up, they bowed to Charles's coffin in the front, and acknowledged President Kibaki effusively. When Cindy and I went up to speak, I didn't bow to Charles, I patted his coffin. (I then wondered if I had offended a culture that I respect and love, but some other later speakers also patted his coffin.)

Cindy spoke first. Her topic was "Choose to Live a Life that Matters," based on the poem by Michael Josephson, that ends by noting that living a life that matters doesn't happen by accident. Charles Mwangi chose to live a life that mattered.

Not having thought about or prepared any comments for President Kibaki until faced with the fact that he was sitting right there and everyone else was acknowledging him, I got around that problem by prefacing my remarks by saying, "President Kibaki has many titles, but today, his title is 'Friend of Charles.'"

As a tribute to Charles, I have chosen to end this book with the words I spoke that day.

GOODBYE TO CHARLES

All of our lives are stories—from Moses to Jesus to the smallest, briefest life. Some life stories are more interesting than others. Charles Mwangi Gathuri's story is exceedingly interesting—and because this brilliant man had a finely honed sense of humor, it was also funny. His story is filled with many characters. Those of us gathered here today are among those characters. Some of us played starring roles, starting with his wonderful, beautiful wife, Charity, and his children of whom he was so proud. They are Betty, Tony and his wife Josephine, Wandia and her husband Steve. His beloved grandchildren are Kui, BuBu, and Matthew.

[His namesake grandson, Charlie, was born to Wandia and Steve after his death.]

The rest of us played varying roles in his story, the best of which were entitled, "Friend of Charles." These friends are scattered around the world. Three of us here today represent his great number of friends in the United States: Cindy Candler, Katherine Davey, and myself, Kemie Nix. Cindy Candler and Katherine Davey represent First Presbyterian Church of Atlanta and its pastor, George Wirth, who was a friend of Charles and, indeed, of all Kenya. Cindy is an old and dear friend of the Mwangis, who has stayed with them many times across the years while helping build up Mount Kenya Academy. Among her many gifts is everyone's favorite, Grace Chapel. Katherine Davey's gift, Chaka

Presbyterian Church, can be seen while driving down the Mwangis' driveway.

Other people whom we are honored to represent are the people, past and present, of The Westminster Schools of Atlanta, which is the sister school of Mount Kenya Academy. Outstanding among these friends are the Hawkins Family, Susan, Scott, Sarah, and Carter. By helping Mount Kenya Academy, they are friends of Kenya's children, both at the school, in the larger community, and those of future generations.

All this help toward the future of Kenya rests squarely on the shoulders of Charles and Charity. Charles had the good sense to marry a visionary educator. While his idea of a good education was his own—battered into his head by tough Irish Catholic Fathers—he always supported Charity's educational ideals, high academic standards with many enriching activities—and no battering. Charles opened his wallet at strategically important junctions of development, especially by buying Nyeri Kindergarten to launch his young wife's educational dreams.

Mount Kenya Academy grew rapidly. Charity Mwangi visited The Westminster Schools of Atlanta and invited an ever-expanding stream of American visitors into their home—including me. Charles was a wonderful, teasing host. As I grew to know him, I learned that he was a serious man, but one who never said a serious thing. Once, he decided that I needed to see his cows. He explained to me that as an

African man, cows were important to him. After inquiring whether I knew about cows, he said, "We better take sticks."

He armed himself and me with strong sticks, and we hiked off. I was sure that we were going to face raging bulls. Instead, we met the most benign cows that I have ever seen. I said, "Charles, these are *JERSEYS*." (My daughter had lived on the Isle of Jersey, and they were the only breed of cows that I could recognize.) Later, when one of these sweet cows was sick, Charles said that the only veterinarian available was Catholic. Did I suppose he would treat a Presbyterian cow?

Charles loved his country and served it well. One of his many and mostly unsung good deeds was starting the development of water tanks as gifts to government schools. A wonderful African-American author and illustrator, Ashley Bryan, visited Mount Kenya Academy and many government schools. He wanted to give water tanks to remote Kiboya Primary School. Charles undertook this task, driving there many times to supervise their installation. Who but Charles would know how to purchase big, black plastic water tanks in Nairobi and have them trucked to the school and installed on concrete platforms complete with guttering on the buildings to capture rainwater? Other water tanks that have been donated to other government schools are built on the firm foundation laid by Charles Mwangi.

In Matthew 10:42, Jesus said, "And whosoever gives one of these little ones even a cup of cold water to drink because he is a disciple, I solemnly tell you that he will not lose his reward."

Mount Kenya Academy would not exist without the lives of Charles and Charity Mwangi. Because they *have* lived, future generations of children will receive an excellent education. Their influence on the lives of individuals, on Kenya, and indeed, all of Africa is incalculable. While this book sadly ends with the death of Charles, his work will live. The influence of his wife, Charity Mwangi, the founder of Mount Kenya Academy, will be an ever-lengthening shadow into the future.

Books mentioned in the text

Adamson, Joy. *Born Free: A Lioness of Two Worlds.* Collins & Harvill, 1960.

Adamson, Joy. *Living Free: The Story of Elsa and her Cubs.* Harcourt, 1961.

Alexander, Lloyd. *Time Cat: The Remarkable Journeys of Jason and Gareth.* Holt, 1963.

Alexander, Lloyd. *Westmark.* Turtleback, 2002.

Blixen, Karen. *Out of Africa.* Modern Library, 1992.

Bryan, Ashley. *Beautiful Blackbird.* Atheneum, 2003.

Curtis, Christopher Paul. *Bud, Not Buddy.* Delacorte, 1999.

Epstein, Samuel. *Harriet Tubman: Guide to Freedom.* Garrard, 1968.

Frankel, Marvin E., and Ellen Saideman. *Out of the Shadows of Night: The Struggle for International Human Rights.* Delacorte, 1989.

Livingston, Myra. *There Was a Place and Other Poems.* McElderry, 1988.

Markham, Beryl. *West with the Night.* North Point, 1983.

Paterson, Katherine. *The Great Gilly Hopkins.* HarperCollins, 1987.

Staples, Suzanne. *Shabanu: Daughter of the Wind.* Knopf, 1989.

Williams, John. *A Field Guide to the Birds of East Africa.* Collins, 1989.

Wells, Rosemary. *McDuff Moves In.* Hyperion, 1997.

Acknowledgments

Special thanks to Mary Hollowell for serving as a reader and editor of this book in its early stages.

Deepest gratitude goes to Margaret Quinlin, the publisher of Peachtree Publishers. She not only published this book, she served as its kind and patient editor.

Thank you also to the wonderful team from Peachtree Publishers who helped immeasurably: Elyse Vincenty, Vicky Holifield, Nicola Simmonds Carmack, and Melanie McMahon Ives.

I cannot even begin to thank all of the unsung volunteers of the various programs of Children's Literature for Children. Nevertheless, on behalf of the children you have helped, and on my own behalf, I thank you from a grateful heart.

Ashley Bryan and Kemie Nix in front of her library plaque

KEMIE NIX has dedicated her professional life to children and books. For a number of years, she taught at The Westminster Schools in Atlanta, Georgia. Allowing her passion to propel her into making a difference in education, she created a reading program that used children's literature in the classroom to inspire a love for reading in her students. Seeing its success, she was invited to implement the program in other schools in Atlanta and abroad, including Mount Kenya Academy; traveling back and forth, she continued her role as a book teacher for over thirty years. She lives in Georgia.